MW00616677

Towards

Meaningful Prayer

Towards Meaningful Prayer

Inspiring Thoughts & Stories on Tefilah from Classic Sources

by S. Feldbrand

Published by
Lishmoa Lilmod U'lelamed

לעילוי נשמת אבי ומורי
ר' יהושע אלי' בן ר' חיים שאול גראסמאן ע"ה
אשר הרבה פעל בהדפסת והפצת ספרים
על טהרת הקדש. ספר זה מוקדש לנשמתו
הטהורה שתעלה מעלה מעלה בגן עדן.

לע"נ ר' מרדכי בן אברהם יודה ווים ע"ה
עמוד החסד ודבוק בצדיקים כל ימי חייו.

ולעילוי כל הנשמות שאין להם מליץ יושר תנצב"ה

Tel. 276 - 9886

Rabbi P. Hirschprung
230 Querbes
Montreal, Quebec

I was shown a book in English by Rebbetzin Feldbrand, relating to the topic of tefilah. She has assembled material which is certain to inspire its readers to heightened worship of Hashem, so that they are more acutely aware before Whom they stand in prayer.

The various concepts on the power and importance of tefilah are sure to make prayers more meaningful for all. May Hashem accept our prayers for general and particular salvation.

We should all merit to behold the Bais Hamikdash in its glory, in compassion, speedily in our days.

Translation of Rabbi Hirschprung's zt"l approbation to
a previous edition of this sefer.

Table of Contents

PREFACE

This book is for people who want to infuse their prayers with more meaning and heighten their awareness that they are communicating directly with Hashem. Its purpose is to expand our knowledge of the far-reaching effects of our prayer. Keep it handy, and consult it before davening. The techniques recorded in this volume will enable you to summon the wherewithal to daven with renewed focus. For maximum benefit, read no more then a few pages at a time.

No entry is original. I have only collected and translated the words of our Sages, systematizing the material for the reader's benefit as a curator arranges paintings for an exhibit. Mastering its contents will enable you to wield the most potent weapon we have, for survival and spiritual growth. Now, more than ever, we see that "we have no one to rely on but our Father in Heaven," (Sota 9,15). It is therefore imperative that we do everything, in our power, to improve communication with Him. I can only hope that this treasury of thoughts will improve your davening as they have mine. May we thus merit the imminent redemption of our beleaguered people.

ACKNOWLEDGEMENTS

First I would like to thank Professor A. Boyarsky for allowing me to use the Tefilah manuscript compiled from my classes, by the students of Ohel Sorah Seminary.

In addition I am indebted to the thousands of students I taught at Torah and Vocational Institute, for enabling me to crystallize many of the thoughts cited in this Sefer.

Words can not properly express my appreciation to Rochel Sanders for helping give this book its final shape.

My deep gratitude to Haim Sherrf who gave generously of his time and graciously allowed me to use his painting for the book's cover.

My thanks to Elky Langer for her professional and pleasant editing of this manuscript.

I am grateful to Leah Schechter for typesetting and to Yehuda Kops for proofreading, and to both for the finishing touches on this sefer.

* * * * * * *

To my husband Mayer, for having made me an "Eishes Chaver".

To my mother, the pillar of strength of our family.

To my in-laws, righteous descendants of illustrious forebears.

To my children, for helping me with sources and sharing the computer with me. May they and their children continue to grow in Torah and Yiras Shamayim until 120.

To Hashem Yisborach, for the privilege of serving Him.

S. Feldbrand
Montreal
Shevat 5763 / January 2003

INTRODUCTION

The Need for Structured Prayer

There are two categories of prayer: innate, subconscious communication; and structured, formal devotions. Everyone, even one who has never opened a prayer book, finds that at times their heart instinctively formulates words of prayer, in a spontaneous outpouring of the soul. Something inside us impels man to pray, and our lips begin unconsciously mumbling a prayer.

This prayer may be associated with a sigh of relief, as in the "Thank G–d" that follows release from a period of intense anxiety. Or it may be a heartfelt request, "Please, Hashem, make her well"; or a plea for intervention, "Please help me succeed." Sometimes prayer is verbalized in response to the feeling of awe and admiration we experience when viewing vast oceans, breathtaking mountains, stunning deserts. It can also be an expression of uplifted emotion, when we comprehend a soul-stirring concept or when a melody touches our very essence. A heartfelt "Thank You" for a period of grace is also prayer.

R' Shlomo Zalmen Auerbach would never repeat any part of his prayer. He prayed slowly and deliberately, as if he were adding up a pile of coins. One day the members of his family noticed him repeating the second paragraph of Birkas Hamazon. They asked him why he had repeated it. He explained that the first time he had said the words of ''nodeh lecha" he hadn't been concentrating properly. "To say 'thank you' without paying attention is 'no thank you'," he concluded.

A groan can also be an expression of a prayer and uplifted to the service of Hashem. Another type of prayer is: "How sorry I am," the confession of a person who has qualms of conscience about a wrong he has done. And finally, when a man stands bewildered in the midst of the mighty Universe, and calls to his Father in Heaven to help him in his struggle and give him direction; this, too, is prayer.

These types of prayers are all indications of our G—dly consciousness. When we are feeling fragile in a relentless world swirling with challenges, when we are seized with great spasms of emotion that churn upwards, our soul instinctively turns to its source for comfort.

If a man was climbing a ladder, with his friend standing below, and the ladder began to sway, he would cry out to his friend to save him. He knows his friend is there; he knows he will help him. We must call out to Hashem in times of need, for we count on His salvation to support the ladder, so to speak, so we do not fall.[1]

The Chofetz Chaim began to speak directly to Hashem when he was left an orphan. It became his habit to turn to Hashem for anything he was lacking. He would take his Tehillim, stand in a corner, and begin conversing with Hashem.

When he was older, he would go up to his attic when everyone was asleep and confer with Hashem. He would start by thanking Hashem for all the good that he received, specifying each and every incident. He felt unworthy of Hashem's compassion. But when he was promoting the welfare of the Jewish people, his tone would become more demanding. He would recount all the good the Jewish people had done. Then, his voice choking with tears, he would describe the suffering they endured and beg Hashem to put an end to all their sorrows.

He would recommend that a person talk to Hashem like one would talk to a mother, knowing that she is there to help him; with the confidence of a child who knows that even if he asks again and again, his mother will not get angry.

Rav Yisrael Zev Gustman was advised by the Tchebiner Rav to purchase an expensive new building for his yeshiva. Knowing how difficult it would be to raise the funds neces-

sary for the purchase, Rav Gustman decided to go to the Kosel to discuss his problem with Hashem.

"We know that Yiftach in his generation is like Shmuel in his generation. The Tchebiner Rav, a leader of this generation, says I should buy the building in Rechavia priced at one hundred and fifty thousand dollars. You know better than I do what is in the bank. So I want to know – why should one hundred fifty thousand be any more difficult for You than the forty thousand the less expensive building costs?"

After a moment's pause, Rav Gustman continued, "Silence is consent." He followed the advice of the Tchebiner Rav, and within two days his son-in-law had miraculously raised all the money that was needed.

Putting it into Words

"Why isn't it enough to frame a prayer in my heart and communicate with Hashem through my thoughts?" people ask.

When a person's prayer remains only in his thoughts and reflections, it is unclear and incomplete. Words translate ideas and desires into physical realities, giving form to the intentions of the heart. Verbalizing one's feelings also gives the individual a better understanding of his true inner self. He is then better able to relate both to himself, and to his Creator.

Since prayer is the innermost longing of the soul, it should be expressed in the form that is most representative of our superior capabilities – speech.[2]

Tefilah is a uniquely human function. More than any other ability, the faculty of intelligent speech sets human beings apart from the animals. It is through speech that man can praise Hashem, study Torah, and unite with others to serve Hashem. It is therefore appropriate that verbal prayer be our means of communicating with Hashem, reminding us of our mission on earth as His servants.

Articulating the words is important because actually hearing the words we utter keeps our thoughts from straying. Even when we recite the words, our thoughts tend to wander. If we prayed only by *thinking*, this tendency would increase, and it would be exceedingly difficult to focus.[3] People have related that speaking to Hashem aloud makes it easier to internalize the fact that Hashem is listening to our prayers, and this makes their prayers more meaningful.

Prayerful thoughts impact the soul, but it is the words of prayer, said aloud, that spread their radiance throughout the body. Uttering the holy words empowers them with enough additional energy to recharge our physical frame.[4]

The Spinka Rebbe, the Chakal Yitzchak, would repeat the words of the prayer "Ve'haer Einenu Be'Sorasecha" (enlighten our eyes with Your Torah) again and again, with tears and anguished outpouring that would move a heart of stone. Each time he repeated the words, his voice became louder and stronger, until it became a roar that resounded like a clap of thunder.

Anyone who witnessed this emotional display immediately understood how the Rebbe had merited Divine revelations in Torah and fear of G–d. After such impassioned prayer, all obstacles to saintliness surely evaporated. (*Marbitzei Torah Me'Olam Ha'Chassidus*)

The Right Words

Occasionally, spontaneous *tefilah* comes easily to our lips. More often, however, we find that we simply don't know what to say or how to say it. Formulating the right words is an art. It is difficult to express our innermost feeling. Because emotions are variable and affected by circumstances such as health, success or failure, we often feel distanced from Hashem.

Yet our needs remain the same, whether we are momentarily uplifted or emotionally depressed. The heart continues to crave G–d as a baby does its mother. If one day the baby's voice is hoarse and he cannot call out for his mother, does he need her any less?

There may be times when we are having trouble earning a living. We will pray for assistance in that area and forget to pray for our health and general welfare. Perhaps there is a war going on, so a person's mind is concerned with that and he forgets to pray for his livelihood. Our Sages established a form for prayer which includes all of our standard requirements, to ensure that each person will always pray for all of his needs.

Even a healthy man must pray for health, and a wealthy man for his livelihood, for our lives are not secure. Our health and our livelihood are not in our own hands. We have no way of knowing what the future holds. It is possible for a rich man to lose his wealth, and a healthy man may become ill. One prays also for continued good health and fortune.

Perhaps on a certain day we would not ask for additional perception, but the words of the *Shemoneh Esrei* remind us to do so. If we would wait until each Jew keenly feels the bitterness of exile to cry out "redeem us," many would never come to utter the words of the blessing of redemption.

Although rain is an important objective, would physicians, lawyers or accountants remember to ask for it? Even if the individual remembers to make all the numerous requests for himself, would he remember to pray for the well- being of others? By following the form of the prayer book, we learn to put our own requests in perspective and enlarge the range of our concerns. Our sages formulated prayer to include all of man's requirements, to prevent any lapses in our prayers.[5]

The Language of Prayer

According to the Mishnah, those who do not know *Lashon HaKodesh* (the Holy Tongue) are permitted to pray in any language they understand. Grace after Meals may be said in any language as well, except for Aramaic.[6] Later halachic authorities advocated that prayers be said in the Holy Tongue.[7] If one prays in the Holy Tongue, one fulfills his obligation even if he does not understand what he is saying.[8]

It has been the custom of all Jewish communities from time immemorial to *daven* only in the Holy Tongue. Our prayers then link our thoughts and desires with the yearnings of Jews all over the world, uniting us throughout the generations. Historically, any Jewish community that severed its bond with the Holy Tongue ultimately disappeared through intermarriage and assimilation. "It is not fitting that we *daven* and weave the crown of the life of worlds in any language other than the Holy Tongue with which the universe was created." *(Kanfei Yonah)*

Lashon Hakodesh is not only a communication tool; it has great metaphysical value as a repository of the Divine mystery. Prayers in other languages cannot be compared to *davening* in the Holy Tongue, whose very words stand in the highest places of the universe.[9] Only the Holy Tongue allows for the interchange of letters and multilevel readings. Even the accents with which the words are read are of great philosophical importance.[10]

The twenty-two letters of the *aleph bais* were created before everything else. These sacred letters contain profound spiritual concepts. With them, Hashem created all the worlds. Each arrangement of letters resulted in a new blend of cosmic forces. When the letters were combined into words, phrases and commands, they brought about the whole of Creation. The task of man is to link with these letters. If we succeed, our prayers join the constant flow which energizes creation, readily rising to its source.[11]

The formal prayers composed by the Men of the Great Assembly were the result of the combined input of 120 holy men, including prophets. These men incorporated the body of esoteric knowledge into the holy words of our prayers.[12] As a microcosm of all created entities, man is able to inspire all living things. When a person utters the words of prayer properly, all creation joins with him in prayer. Even the song of a passing bird may enter into man's prayer, uniting with him to praise Hashem.[13]

The *Chidah*, Rabbi Chayim Yosef David Azulai, writes that the combination of letters, as formulated by the men of Great Assembly, have the power to arouse forces beyond our imagination. When we articulate our prayers, the sacred letters connect to their spiritual roots. Thus energized, they interact with the circumstances prevailing on earth at that instant, resulting in unprecedented spiritual achievements.[14]

Raban Gamliel had to seek out a great man to compose the nineteenth blessing of the Amidah, known as HaMinim. Simply writing a few lines in the holy tongue does not require much expertise. But knowledge of the secret combinations required to formulate a blessing, which would impact the heavenly strata and weaken the forces of evil, required great wisdom and holy spirit.

One who uses a proper telescope can see the stars. The letters of *tefilah* form such lenses, which can be used to perceive the hidden ways of Hashem. One who has developed spiritual sensibility can feel the greatness of Hashem when he says the words "the great"; he can see the power of Hashem in the words "the powerful"; the awe of Hashem in the words "the awesome." The letters have the power to draw forth these qualities from above.[15]

Nevertheless, a person should learn the meaning of prayers in his own vernacular, for prayer must be understood.[16] Since prayer is the way the heart communicates, if the heart does not understand what the mouth utters, then the prayer is of little value.[17] It is impossible to pray with feeling unless one understands what he is saying.[18] Understanding the words we say facilitates concentration.[19] It also makes prayer more enjoyable. A person who is thoroughly familiar with the prayers will delight in the structure and nuances of everything he says.[20]

> *While staying overnight at a hotel, Rabbi Yechezkel Abramsky awoke one morning to a voice praying in the next room. The unbelievably sweet voice was saying the prayer "Nishmas" word for word, followed by a translation into Yiddish. After overhearing those words brimming with emotion, R' Yechezkel found that he could no longer sleep. Later he discovered that he had overheard the Chofetz Chaim communicating with Hashem.*

Our goal is to learn how to put our whole head and heart into our daily *davening*, so each verse and every phrase comes alive.

Once we reach that spiritual plateau, our thrice-daily time with Hashem will be the highlight of our day and the delight of our existence. While spontaneous prayer requires no priming, maximizing our structured time with Hashem requires meaningful effort to transport our thoughts to elevated spiritual spheres.

[1] Shearim Be'Tefila, Bitzur

[2] Nesivos Olam

[3] Magen Abraham, 101, 2

[4] Zach Ve'Naki, Chapter two

[5] Prayer, Rabbi Azariah Hildeshiemer

[6] Sotah 7,1

[7] Mishnah Berurah, Aruch Ha'Shulcahn to Orach Chayim chapters 62 and 101

[8] Biur Halacha, Orach Chayim 62,3

[9] Nefesh Ha'Chayim 2:13 in note

[10] Kuzari 2, 72

[11] Or Ha'Emes 36b

[12] Nefesh Ha'Chayim 2,10

[13] Darchei Tzedek 6b, Tzavaas Baal Shem Tov

[14] Shem Ha'Gedolim on Rabbi Yitzchak of Acco

[15] Shemuah Tovah 73b

[16] Sefer Chasidim 588

[17] Rashi, Sotah 33a

[18] Kanfei Yona

[19] Noheg Ka'tzone Yosef page 40

[20] Shearim Be'Tefilah, Chilui

The Essence of Prayer

Speaking with Hashem

Hashem invites man to pray to Him: "Call unto me and I will answer you." (*Yirmiyah 33:9*) Rabbi Zeira adds: When a man has a visitor, the first time he seats him on a couch; the second on a chair; the third on a bench. By the fourth time he grumbles, "How much longer is he going to disturb me?" But Hashem eternally awaits our prayers. As soon as we address Him, He is eager to respond to us.[1]

Hashem takes joy in our continual prayers. Whereas man would resent repeated requests, Hashem wants to hear from us.[2] Each time we approach Hashem, our connection with Him is strengthened. When we approach a friend for a favor, we hope that he will grant our wish — and that we will not have to approach him again. With prayer, however, each appeal to Hashem is significant and noteworthy.

Rabbi Levi Yitzchak of Berditchev once observed Jews praying hurriedly. After they had finished praying, R' Levi

Yitzchak called over two of the younger ones. "I have question," he said. "Ma, Ma, Ma, Na, Na, Na?"

"What's that you're saying?" the merchants asked.

Rabbi Levi Yitzchak continued mumbling, "Ba, Ba, Ba, Ta, Ta, Ta." They looked at him, uncomprehending.

"What's the problem?" replied Rabbi Levi Yitzchak. "Don't you understand what I'm saying? Wasn't that exactly the way you prayed?"

"When an infant in its crib murmurs ba and ma, not even the greatest wise men in the world know what the infant is talking about," said one of the merchants. "Yet the child's parents immediately know what the child wants – whether it is hungry or thirsty or wet. We Jews are the children of Hashem, and Hashem understands what we are asking for and hears our prayers."

"You answered well," R' Levi Yitzchok exclaimed. "Our Father in heaven will surely receive the prayers of His children." And he began dancing with joy. (Toldos Kedushas Levi)

Our Sages[3] highlight the contrast between a human king and the King of all Kings. "For which great nation has a G–d Who is close to it, as is Hashem, our G-d, whenever we call to Him?" (Devarim 4,7) Hashem immediately responds to any request in any language.[4]

In former times, when a man wished an audience with the king, he had to make an appointment well in advance. He would have to wait patiently as the months passed, counting *the weeks and then the days until the date of the rendez-vous. When the long expected day finally arrived, the man would don an outfit tailored especially for this momentous occasion and proceed with great exultation to the palace of the king.*

Suppose the king's secretary informed him that the king was not receiving anyone because he does not feel well. The man would be devastated. He would protest, "Today is my appointment with the king. I have been waiting for months for this day."

"Nothing can be done. The king is sick. He is not receiving anyone today – not even his children."

How heartsick the man would feel, having his dreams shattered after so many months of eager anticipation. The tears begin to fall. He is incapable of restraining them. Where will he turn now?

He tells himself that even if the king would have received him, he had no guarantee that the king would have granted his request that day. Possibly he would have summarily rejected his plea and had him thrown out of his presence in disgrace.

He feels thoroughly dejected. Will he be able to get another appointment? Can he wait that long? What will be his fate now?

We don't need an appointment with Hashem. We don't have to buy a new garment. A person need only begin speaking and specify his needs. Hashem is there beside us listening. He loves us, is ready to help us, and can find solutions to problems that seem impossible to solve. Just as He has helped us many times in the past, He can help us now.[5]

When we petition Hashem for aid, the request is more significant than the response. Being able to praise Hashem is a greater gift than life, as the Malbim explains the verse in Tehillim 63, "Then I shall bless you all my life."

A man spent a long time looking for a specialist to cure his chronic ailment. To his great joy, he located a doctor who was able to make him well. The doctor he discovered happened to be a very nice person, and the two of them became fast friends.

There are two benefits we gain from prayer. We strengthen our relationship with Hashem, and we benefit by having our prayers answered. In fact, it is our fellowship with Hashem which is the more valuable of the two.

Shaul *Hamelech* went out to seek donkeys and found a kingdom.[6] We open our Siddur and make our mundane requests, only to discover a kingdom – the joy of spiritual closeness to Hashem.[7]

Prayer: Our Most Important Effort

When Nechemiah approached the king for permission to rebuild Yerushalayim, he said, "And I prayed to the G–d of Heaven, and I said to the king, 'If the king would be so kind to send me to Yehudah so that I may rebuild it.'" *(Nechemiah 2, 4-5)* Interestingly enough, the verse gives no further details about Nechemiah's prayer to G–d. The *Ramah Me'Pano* explains that his petition to the king was his prayer. He was applying for permission from the earthly ruler, but in his heart he was praying to Hashem to fulfill that request.

Many believe that after doing what they can to reach their goal, they should turn to Hashem to do the rest. This is an erroneous perception. We do not do half, while Hashem does the other half; Hashem actually does it all. Our efforts are merely a screen to cover the deeds of Hashem. We should not deceive ourselves into believing that there is a correlation between our efforts and the ultimate results. Only our prayers have true substance. When we have internalized this concept, we can then pray effectively.[8]

In 1939, Jews living in Germany who were natives of Poland were delivered to the Polish border. R' Moshe Leib Schneider, head of Yeshivas Toras Moshe, was one of the exiles. While others were bemoaning their status and worrying what the future would bring, Rabbi Schneider was busy analyzing which city would be the best for starting a yeshiva, Vilna, Warsaw or Lodz?

When he arrived at the border of Poland, he discovered that it was closed. He returned to Frankfurt and resumed teaching. A few days later, the yeshiva was closed by the Gestapo. Most of his students crowded together into his small apartment so they could continue their studies. They studied all day, davened with many tears, shared their meals, and slept on the floor, waiting for the day they could flee Germany.

The Nazis could be heard one day searching for Jews. The boys wanted to block the door with the furniture, but R' Moshe stopped them. "That will not save us," he said. They said Tehillim with heart-rending cries. The Nazis arrived at their doorstep, but a non-Jewish neighbor told them that all the Jews in that building were gone, and they moved on...

When R' Moshe was convinced that there was no possibility of spiritual accomplishments in that cursed land, he agreed to leave. As a result of the efforts of Rabbi Yechezkel Abramsky and Reb Aharon Goodman, he received a visa to England in the last days before war broke out. When he arrived, he immediately opened a yeshiva.

His difficulties did not end in England. When the Germans invaded France, the British government decided to incarcerate all those born in Germany or Austria for fear that there were spies among them. Forty students, about half of Rabbi Schneider's yeshiva, were exiled to a distant island. At the instigation of unscrupulous individuals, the government decided to close the yeshiva. After many attempts to have this decree annulled, it was decided that the yeshiva could continue to function, but R' Moshe had to join the others who had been banished to the island.

R' Moshe declared a fast on behalf of the yeshiva. Everyone prayed with all their might. A few days later, representatives of the crown paid a visit to Chief Rabbi Hertz to look into the situation. The Chief Rabbi did a marvelous job of defending the righteous Rabbi Schneider, and his words were well received. As a result, the yeshiva was no longer viewed with suspicion. (Marbitzei Torah U'Mussar)

Prayer is our secret weapon. "They by chariots and they by horses, while we call out the name of Hashem." *(Tehillim 20)* After we have prayed, we are empowered to do what has to be done.[9]

This concept can be explained by citing an incident that occurred in 1948 in the presence of the Brisker Rav. Some individuals who were close to him seemed very impressed by the prowess of the Israeli army. The Brisker Rav felt that it was important that they know that it was not the guns, the explosives, the tanks or the planes that won the war. It was the Psalms, the prayers and the entreaties of the righteous ones that overcame the enemy.

As far as the Jewish people are concerned, the theater of war is not in the air, on the ground or at sea, but in the heavens alone. There the ground rules are simple. Have the prayers been accepted? Who will prevail, the accusing angels on one side, or repentance and good deeds on the other? What occurs below is child's play. Actions below must be performed to the best of our ability, but the objectives will be attained by righteous individuals such as R' Zeev Zaitchek, R' Shlomo Bloch and others like them.

When the Rav was asked why so many were killed despite the prayers of these great people, he related an incident that had occurred with his grandfather. When the Bais Halevi's son became engaged, his father was displeased at his son's delight with the large dowry he was to receive. The father said to his son, "You did not receive that dowry as a result of your good deeds, but only because you are my son."

The son denied that claim, asserting that if it were really in his father's merit, the amount would have been far higher. His father did not deny the point, but emphasized that the final lower sum reflected the fact that it was the son who was the chosson.

The Brisker Rav explained that the prayers of the righteous should have ensured that there were no deaths. Yet the

Zionists were also enmeshed in the events. The reason people were killed was because of the secular ideology of the Zionists. Their belief that their weapons and planes resulted in victory, was responsible for the casualties.

Guaranteed Results

"The eyes of all look to You with hope and You give them their food in its proper time," *(Tehillim 145,15).* What is the proper time? A person whose confidence in Hashem is unconditional is guaranteed that all his supplications will eventually be granted.

Even if our requests are not answered immediately, we should retain our optimism that our prayers will achieve results. It may take time, but Hashem will definitely respond. As our Sages tell us, a prayer may be answered after forty days, after twenty days, after three days, or after one day. Some prayers may be answered that day, that hour, or that moment. There are prayers that have not even been articulated and are already answered.[10]

Moshe Rabbeinu looked into the future and promoted the efficacy of prayer on behalf of his descendants. He said, "Master of the Universe, when you see Your sons in anguish and there is no one to plead for compassion on their behalf, immediately answer them." The Holy One replied, "Moshe, by your life, I will answer their prayers whenever they call to me."[11]

King David prayed, "Master of the Universe, do not repudiate the generations that have no king, no prophet, no Priest and no *Urim Ve'Tumim.*"[12] He ensured that Hashem would process our requests until the coming of *Mashiach.*

It is possible for a man to determine if his prayer has been accepted, writes the Baal Shem Tov. When a person finds that his heart is being directed in the right way, and he prays without any extraneous thoughts, with love and reverence, then he knows that Hashem will accept his prayer.[13]

If a person is happy after praying, this is another indication that he will be answered. The opposite is true if he is depressed.[14]

When Rabban Gamliel's son fell seriously ill, he sent two sages to Rabbi Chanina to pray for his recovery. Rabbi Chanina was widely known for the miracles that Hashem performed through him. It was a well-known fact that his tefillos were dear to Hashem and accepted willingly. As soon as Rabbi Chanina spoke with the two Sages, he quickly ran up to the loft of his house and prayed with great kavana that the fever should subside and the boy recover. Meanwhile, the messengers waited nervously downstairs. When he came back down, he said to them, "Go in peace, for the fever has left the boy."

The two were astounded. "But how do you know that? Who told you?"

Rabbi Chanina replied, "I am neither a prophet, nor the son of a prophet, but I have a tradition from my grandfather that if a prayer runs smoothly, it is a sign that it has been heard. My prayer just now went smoothly, without any hindrance. I am therefore sure that it was heard."

The two men noted down the time that Rabbi Chanina informed them of the patient's recovery. When they returned to the home of Rabban Gamliel, they were told that this was the very time when the fever left his son. (Berachos 34)

Persistent Prayer

"A person who prays a lot will have his prayers answered." *(Berachos 32)* The fact that we pray again and again is an indication that we truly rely on Hashem to save us. Even if a person is unworthy of having his prayers answered, if he prays and begs Hashem to help, Hashem will have compassion in the merit of his confidence in Him.[15]

If a person prays and is not answered, he should not lose faith and he should not be discouraged. He should pray again, as it says, "Yearn for Hashem, strengthen your heart and yearn for Hashem." *(Tehillim 27, 140)*

If we knew a government official could save the life of a loved one, we would repeatedly attempt to persuade him to help us. We would not rest until we had reached our goal. Our prayers must be approached in the same manner, with the knowledge that we have no other recourse.[16]

When a person is experiencing a crisis, he will run far and near in search of assistance. The Chazon Ish recommends focusing on repentance, prayer and charity. Hashem will certainly fulfill his request.[17]

One of the languages of prayer is *VaYifgah*.[18] One possible etymology of this word is "*Pega*," which means a pest.[19] R' Dovid of Lelov explains the word *VaYifgah* as "and he pestered." An effective means of prayer is to repeat our request again and again.[20]

Pray to Hashem to fortify your resolve to keep praying until your prayers are answered.[21] Recognize that your prayers are never burdensome nor annoying.[22]

"*Chaneni Hashem ki eilecha ekrah kol hayom* – Have compassion, Hashem, for to You I call all the day." *(Tehillim 86,3)*

A father will ignore a son's request if he is convinced that the boy will soon tire and stop badgering him. It is up to the child to convince his father that what he wants is so important to him, that he will not give up his nudging. With the above verse, we tell Hashem that we will not tire – we will keep crying out to Him all day. Surely, then, Hashem will listen to our prayers. (Arvei Nachal Parsha Vaereh)

The gates of Heaven are not always open. If you repeat your prayers often enough, however, at one point you will find the doors open, and your wishes will be granted.[23]

Why aren't we told when these moments of heavenly grace will occur? So we will not neglect our prayers at all other times.[24]

Yitzchak and Rivkah knew that frequent prayers would ultimately achieve their intended goal. *Rashi* teaches us that they *davened* repeatedly and at great length.[25]

A King once asked his son to transfer an extremely large stone to the tower of the palace. No matter how the prince tried, he could not figure out a way to lift such a huge stone, let alone get it up to the tower. Finally, the king said, "Do you really think I expect you to carry it in one piece? Chip away at the stone with a chisel and hammer, and each day bring up the pieces. Eventually the entire stone will have been brought up to the tower." (Tzadik #441)

Moshe Rabbeinu kept praying for forty days until Hashem forgave the Jews for the sin of the golden calf. Numerous commentaries point out that he prayed again and again. They emphasize that praying again and again is more effective than a single lengthy prayer.[26]

According to the *Baal Haturim*, Moshe Rabbeinu made use of all types of prayers when he pleaded with Hashem to permit him to enter the Land of Israel. His prayers were so potent that heaven and earth quaked. Hashem proclaimed that all gates should be shut against the prayers of Moshe, so they would not rise before Him. But Moshe's prayers sliced through the firmaments like a sharp sword, empowered by constant repetition. Many ancient commentaries believe that if Moshe Rabbeinu had persisted in his prayers, Hashem would have permitted his entry to Eretz Yisrael.

Chana prayed again and again.[27] Finally Hashem answered her prayers. When a person prays again and again, each sigh and every tear is collected.[28]

We should make an effort to increase the quality of our prayer each time we repeat it. We will be rewarded for each and every prayer we utter.

The Chofetz Chaim passed a man selling apples at a street corner. He called out loudly to the people walking by, asking them to buy his delicious apples. The passing pedestrians ignored him. Two hours later, the Chofetz Chaim walked past him again. The man was still calling out his wares.

The Chofetz Chaim approached the man. "Reb Yid, I couldn't help noticing your efforts to draw attention to your produce, but I have not seen anyone make a purchase. Are you able to earn a living this way?"

The man replied, "Rebbe, all I know is that when I get home at night, I find that I have earned enough to put food on the table."

The Chofetz Chaim applied this incident to our prayers. We call out to Hashem again and again, and still once more. There is no doubt that Hashem answers. Certainly we are in the same category as this Jew. We must keep calling out our requests. (Meir Einei Yisrael)

A professional couple became religious and switched their children to religious schools. Even their married daughter and son-in-law joined them in their spiritual quest. The father started studying Torah seriously. After five years, he began to spend more time in Kollel and less time pursuing his profession. Finally he resigned from his position and became a full time Kollel man. It was a marvel to behold a man in his fifties learning with the enthusiasm of a young married man.

A family friend explained that from the start it had been the wife's dream that her husband study Torah full time. She felt her dream was a flight of fancy, so preposterous that she did not even broach it to her husband. Instead, she prayed and prayed, said Tehillim countless times, in the hope that her husband might one day become an accomplished Torah scholar. The years passed and her dream became a reality. (Shearim Be'Tefilah, Pegiah)

An added bonus of repeated prayer is that the supplicant becomes permeated with the flavor of those prayers. His very being is altered by the continual repetition of his prayers. He and his prayers become one, so he becomes the epitome of prayer —

just as David Hamelech said of himself, "I am prayer." *(Tehillim 109)*

No Prayer Is Purposeless

Sometimes it appears that our prayers will accomplish nothing. Yet "Prayers and fasts further our interests as well as those of our children." *(Sefer Ha'Chassidim)* Even when they are not answered, our prayers are stored in the upper worlds; each prayer is credited to us in the World to Come.[29]

Sometimes a parent may deny a child's request because it is inappropriate. Still, he will offer the child an alternate favor. Hashem will often do the same. Like a loving parent, Hashem ignores our requests for things that can harm us, but at the same time He confers other benefits upon us which we have not even asked for. This thought should enable us to keep praying even when it appears that our prayers are having no effect.[30]

If you see someone praying unsuccessfully for something you view as desirable, do not conclude that you too will be refused. When R' Akiva saw that the prayers of the great R' Eliezer did not result in rain, he was not discouraged. Ultimately, R' Akiva's prayer was answered.[31]

When Noach left the ark and saw the total devastation, he cried and called out to Hashem, "Master of the Universe, You are called compassionate. You should have had compassion on your creatures!"

Hashem replied, "Now you are crying? You should have cried before the destruction, when you were informed about what would happen."

According to the Imrei Emes, Noach had prayed only on behalf of his family. He had concluded that his generation was unworthy of being saved, because their sins were so grave. But even if a Jew feels his prayers will not be answered, he must make an effort to do what he can with his prayers. If Noach had unleashed the power of prayer on behalf of the generation, they would all have been saved. (Pnei Menachem, Noach 5753)

In Bereishis we are told that Hashem was determined to inform Avraham about what would happen to Sodom. In the next verse, we are told that the reason for telling Avraham was that his descendants would become a great nation.

The Dubno Maggid explains the connection between the verses with a story of two gentlemen who visited a tailor. One was a young father, the other an old man. The old man took his time. He made sure that the measurements were accurate and chose his fabric with care. The younger man made his selection quickly and prepared to leave.

The old man was astonished. "How did they fit you so quickly?" he asked. "I have several teenage sons," the younger man explained. "If the suit doesn't fit me, it will fit one of them."

Hashem knew that Avraham would resolutely pray on behalf of the city. Indeed, Avraham Avinu continued to *daven* on behalf of Sodom even after the angels left to destroy the city.[32] Although his prayers would not be effective then, they would eventually be used by his descendants.[33]

In Avraham's case, it took many generations for his prayers to produce positive results. Only Lot and his two daughters survived the destruction of Sodom and became the progenitors of two enemies of the Jewish people. Many generations later, Ruth, a descendant of this union, became the great-grandmother of King David. Avraham's prayers preserved the antecedent of King David and insured the Davidic dynasty.[34]

The *Steipler* would encourage people to keep *davening* for a sick person even when the situation seemed hopeless. Prayer alleviates the sick person's suffering and lengthens his life . . . and after all, miracles do happen. Prayers will increase the merit of the sick person in this world and the world to come, since he will be rewarded for being the cause of other Jews praying and reaching out to Hashem. Finally, those prayers will save many other people. Only in the world to come is it possible to see all the benefits that resulted from each individual prayer.

When the Brisker Rav, R' Yitzchok Zeev Soloveitchik, would be asked to pray for a sick person, he would first ask for numerous details and make all types of recommendations. He encouraged family members to pursue all medical alternatives, even those that were farfetched. He felt that Hashem's salvation would result from the power of their devotion to the patient and their desire to insure his recovery.

He also advised relatives to refrain from informing others that the patient had improved, as long as the patient was still in danger. He feared that people would stop praying for the patient if they heard good news.

After a petitioner left his room, he would give money to charity and then pray for the sick person with great intensity.

R' Yochanan and R' Elazar said, "Even if a sword's blade is resting on a person's throat, he should never give up praying for Divine mercy, as it says, 'Though He slay me, I would pray to Him.'" *(Iyov 13,15)* R' Chanan said, "Even if an interpreter of dreams tells someone that he will die tomorrow, he should not give up praying for Divine mercy, as it says, "In the multitude of dreams, vanities, and words, you should only fear G–d." *(Koheles 5,6 – Berachos 10)*

The Yavetz recorded the miraculous escape of his grandfather, R' Yaakov, the father of the Chacham Tzvi. In the year 1648, rampaging Cossacks rounded up a large group of Jews, including R' Yaakov. One by one they were slaughtered. When it was the turn of R' Yaakov the murderer exclaimed, "You're too young to die!" He knocked him onto the pile of dead bodies with the handle of his sword. Jews hiding nearby were sure that he had been murdered. When night fell, he pushed his way out of the pile and fled. When the Cossacks were gone, he returned home.

There is no rational way to explain why a bloodthirsty murderer spared him in the heat of the carnage. Hashem has ways of saving a person, even when all seems lost. (Toldos R'Tzvi Hirsch Ashkenazi)

When the Ksav Sofer was six, he was so sick that the name Avraham was added to his name. When his condition worsened, the doctors called for the Chevra Kadisha. They lit candles and began the prayers for the dying.

His father, the Chasam Sofer, walked to the chest where his manuscripts lay and he prayed for his child. At that moment, the feverish child called out, "Shema Yisrael Hashem Elokeinu Hashem Echad."

The doctors examined the child. There was a definite improvement. The members of the Chevra Kadisha extinguished their candles and happily went home. One of the Chasam Sofer's students heard his teacher whisper that he had succeeded in securing fifty years for his son. (Chut Ha'Meshulash)

Bloodthirsty Poles condemned R' Yosef Zundel Salant to death by hanging. He said Viduy as he was led to the gallows. Before they could put the noose around his neck, the Russians entered the city and the Poles fled. (Toldos Ha'Tzaddik R'Yosef Zundel of Salant)

Why Are *Tefilos* Sometimes Not Answered?

Although we are told that all prayers are answered,[35] it seems to us that many requests remain unfulfilled. Though *tefilos* are never rejected, this does not mean that Hashem complies with our total request. He may answer it only partially, or sometimes put it aside, for Hashem knows what is best for us.[36]

Rabbi Yehoshua son of Levi said that Tefilah brings about a fifty percent reprieve. (Va'Yikrah Rabbah, 10,5; Devarim 8,1) When Hashem's anger was aroused against Aharon, he was condemned to lose all four of his children. (Devarim 9,20) Then Moshe davened on behalf of his brother and two of his children were spared. Even though Moshe Rabbeinu was refused entry to Eretz Yisrael, his numerous prayers enabled him to see the land. (Devarim 3, 26-27; 34,10)

The *Steipler* writes that there are some prayers that are answered immediately, and others that are answered after thirty years. Ultimately one will see how much his prayers made a difference. It is impossible for a person to know what his present predicament would have been like had he not prayed; without his prayers, things could have been much worse. Our prayers greatly ease our situation.[37]

It is forbidden to stubbornly demand things of Hashem. We should only request and beg with many petitions and supplications, and Hashem will do what is good. If Hashem means for something to be, he will bring the matter to the best possible conclusion, whether immediately or at a later time.[38]

Sometimes our prayers remain unanswered because Hashem wants them to continue in their intensity. Hashem may delay answering a prayer so a person will become more conscious of his total dependency on Hashem. This will enable him to pray with greater intensity.[39] Sometimes a *tefilah* that seems unanswered has been diverted to fulfill a cosmic need.[40]

Often a person will *daven* faithfully for a specific thing, yet sees no results. He feels that Hashem is not listening. It may very well be that only one prayer is lacking to complete the total of prayers, which will then effect his salvation. Often his deliverance has been arranged, but a little more prayer is required to have it materialize in this world.[41]

A delayed response to our prayers may reflect Hashem's desire to put a person's faith to the test. Hashem purposely fails to answer a person's prayers to determine if he will manifest genuine faith and continue to pray.[42] The frustration we experience when our requests are denied atones for our sins. We are thus spared various punishments.[43]

Hashem may refuse our request because we are asking for something that would harm us. Sometimes we plan to use that which we request for an improper purpose. A prayer may also be rejected if its fulfillment affects others. King David's prayer that he should not die on Shabbos was refused,[44] because it was on that day that his son Solomon's reign was due to begin.

The Talmud Yerushalmi explains why the prayers of the righteous sometimes remain unanswered.

> *There was a king who had two sons. Each of them would present himself to receive spending money from the king. When the first son appeared, his request was granted immediately. The father was annoyed by his presence and ensured that he received what he required at the door, so he would not trouble the king personally.*

> *When the king's second beloved son appeared, the father did not want him to leave quickly. The king delayed granting his request so the son would spend time with him. While the son is in his father's presence, he can feel his father's love so deeply that he does not hesitate to help himself from the royal table. Although both of the sons receive money for expenses, the first son receives his money in shame, while the second brother achieves a closeness to the king which permits him to help himself to what he needs. (Taanis 3,4)*

Occasionally our prayers enable others to find happiness.[45] This was what happened to the prayers of Rochel, who prayed for years to have a child. Her supplications empowered her descendants' prayers. All unanswered, stored prayers will eventually be converted to brilliant illuminations, which will delight the righteous in the world to come.[46] In the next world, the effectiveness of each and every prayer will become apparent.

All *tefillos* are answered, but their answers are often cryptic. Every prayer achieves results, one way or another, sooner or later; for ourselves, or for others.[47] Hashem's reply is not readily discernible as a response to our prayers; it seems to be a natural occurrence. Ultimately, as events evolve, Hashem's intervention becomes evident, as happened during the time of Purim.

The Barrier of Sin

A barrier created by our sins can block the positive response to our prayers. This barrier proclaims that the man has sinned and does not deserve Hashem's compassion. We must repent to the best of our ability, invoking assistance from above to destroy all barriers and circumvent each roadblock.[48] That is why we are told, "A person should never stop evoking compassion, even if a sharp sword is drawn across his throat." *(Tzror Ha'Chayim, three)*

A person who is estranged from the Torah or ignores the cry of the poor will have his requests ignored. Since he does not feel the pain of others, it is fitting that there is no response to his pain. A person who engages in flattery,[49] refuses to accept rebuke,[50] or who slurs and mispronounces words of prayer will find his prayer ignored.[51]

There once lived a man by the name of Azaryah son of Yedidya who was an extremely pious individual, known to be well versed in kabbalah. One night he appeared to his friend Gedalyah in a dream and told him that when his soul was brought aloft for heavenly judgement, he was told to look up at the sky. "I saw what appeared to be countless small flowers. I felt overwhelmed with fear at the sight of these angelic creatures, as numerous as the stars of the heaven. I was told that these are the vowels which I disgraced during the course of my prayers, when I said a tzereh instead of a shvah, or a chirik instead of a shuruk, or when I slurred or skipped a word."

Negative angels created by his mispronunciations were seeking revenge for having been prevented from attaching themselves to the heavenly crown. "If not for my good deeds, my judgment would have been extremely harsh. As it was, I was reincarnated, so I might repair that which I had mangled," he concluded.

As a result of this dream, the community hired a scholar well versed in Hebrew grammar to teach everyone the proper pronunciation of each word. (From a manuscript of R'Mordechai Yaffe as cited in Mateh Yehudah, and Bais Tefilah)

R' Matzliach Mazouz would focus on the deeper meanings of the words of prayer, according to the masters of Kabbalah. One day his students explained to him how their French

teacher had taught them how to distinguish the proper pro-
nunciation of the letter "U," which the boy had been mispro-
nouncing as an "E." The instructor persevered until the boy
had mastered the proper enunciation.

Rabbi Matzliach applied what he had heard to his own
pronunciation of the words of prayer. In Jerba, no one really
emphasized the proper pronunciation of the words. But now
he made a concerted effort to say the words properly. For three
years he labored over his prayers. Ultimately he mastered the
proper pronunciation and it became second nature for him.
(Ish Matzliach)

The *Menoras Hamaor* singles out theft and impure thoughts as
the main deterrents to the acceptance of our prayers.[52] The *Yesod*
Ve'Shoresh Ha'Avodah puts theft at the top of the list of sins
which interfere with the acceptance of our prayers.[53] He also mentions the sins of *shaatnez* and withholding the wage of a day
laborer.[54]

During World War II, when the Mir Yeshiva was in
Shanghai, one of the yeshiva boys suddenly left the shul in the
middle of the Yom Kippur prayers. A short time later he
returned wearing his weekday suit.

After the fast, his friends asked for an explanation. He told
them that his prayers hadn't been going well. He tried to revive
his enthusiasm with the study of Mussar, but nothing helped.
He suddenly remembered that wearing shaatnez was linked to
unsuccessful prayer. Perhaps the suit he was wearing con-
tained shaatnez. So he ran home to change into his weekday
suit, which had been checked for shaatnez in Lithuania. He

was then able to pray with the proper devotion and fervor. When he later gave his Shabbos suit to be checked, he was informed that it contained shaatnez. (Nes Ha'Hatzolah)

A person who benefits from forbidden gain may also find that his prayers are disregarded. The Midrash declares that Iyov said of himself "No injustice is in my hands and my prayer is pure." *(Iyov 16,17)* This implies that both a pure prayer and a sullied prayer exist. The man whose hands are filthied by dishonest gain cries out, yet the Almighty turns away from his prayers – for his plea is tainted. Iyov's prayer was pure, for he was honest, and so his prayers were not rejected.

We say in our Rosh Hashanah prayers, "You are a G–d of truth and Your words are truth." In Heaven, they listen only to words of truth.

A simple unlearned Jew once came to the Kotzker Rebbe to ask whether his daughter should have surgery. The Rav felt that she should not have an operation. Then the man mentioned that he had a smart daughter who felt that surgery would be beneficial.

The Rebbe again replied, " I advise you not to proceed with the surgery."

The man still was not satisfied. He pointed out that his daughter was not only smart but also somewhat knowledge-able in the field of medicine. The Rebbe remained firm in his conviction that the surgery was not desirable.

The give and take continued for a while, with the man insisting that surgery seemed advisable and the Rebbe insist-ing that it was not. As the man took leave of the Rebbe, the

Rebbe asked him if he would follow his advice.

The man replied, "I will see, I need to think about it…" And they parted.

The Rebbetzin had overheard the conversation. She came over to the Rebbe for an explanation. "Your chassidim, who are great men in their own right, travel great distances and wait several hours so they may spent a few moments with you. This simple man merited so much of your time, and you engaged in a seemingly unproductive conversation with him. Why?"

"Why are you so surprised?" the Rebbe replied. "Everything he said was unadulterated truth. He has a sick daughter, that is a fact. He is considering surgery, that is a fact. It is also true that he has a smart daughter who advocates the surgery. Why should I get annoyed with someone who speaks the truth?

"On the other hand, some of my chassidim who visit me try to deceive me with their words. They asked for fear of Heaven, but what they really want is money, health, and sustenance. So a few minutes is enough for them."

A person takes his *siddur* in hand. He has no money to pay his bills; he has serious financial problems. He lowers his head and prays. He begins, "And You are holy," and he thinks *money*; he says, "grant us fear," and he thinks *money*. He continues, "May you reign," and he thinks *money*. He thinks about assets and cash. Is this prayer in truth? It is no wonder that his prayer is denied.

A chassid once asked the Rizhiner why he was still poor when he beseeched Hashem for sustenance in the Kedusha prayers of the Holy Days for so many years. The Rebbe replied that this works only for those who focus on sustenance at that point only, while during the rest of their prayers thoughts of money are forgotten. "Unfortunately, in your case, your entire prayer is focused on money." (Kol Dodi Dofek)

The important thing is to understand that Hashem is not refusing our requests because he wishes us to suffer. Hashem created the world only so that He might allocate goodness in bountiful measure. If Hashem does not fulfill our requests, it might be that we haven't prepared ourselves adequately to receive that which Hashem wants to give us. We should work on improving ourselves so we can become worthy of Hashem's generosity.[54]

1 Midrash Shochar Tov

2 Yismach Lev from Meor Einayim

3 Berachos chap. 9

4 Yalkut Devarim

5 Based on Chovos Ha'levavos: Shaar Ha'Bitachon, and Bitachon Amiti, culled from the writings of Rebbe Nachman of Breslav

6 Shmuel I, chapter s8:10

7 Adapted from Shearim Be'Tefilah, Ittur

8 Adapted from Michtav Me'Eliyahu Part one; Shearim Be'Tefilah, Nipul

9 Lev Shalom

10 Devarim Rabbah 2,10

11 Introduction to Hishtapchus Ha'Nefesh, citing the Zohar

12 Pesikta De'Rav Kahana

13 Toldos Yaakov Yosef BeHalaloscha 138

14 Ibid Ekev 181

15 Tanchumah Vayerah 1

16 Yesodei Ha'daas chapter 48

17 Emunah U'Bitachon chapter two, letter aleph

18 Bereishis 28,11 see Rashi

19 Rashi, Chulin 91

20 Mishlei Chassidim on Torah

21 Menorahs Ha'Maor, light three principle 3; Hischazkus Be'Tefilah Le'Hashem page 30

22 Meiri Yoma 29,1

23 Devarim Rabbah 2,12 based on a verse in Tehilim 69, 14

24 Midrash Agaddah 76, Imrei Pinchas, Shemos; Or Chodosh, Parshas Va'Eschanan

25 Bereishis 25,21

26 Chayei Olam 1,28; Yeshurun 3,395

27 Shmuel 2; 2,12

28 Ralbag, Shmuel 1,7

[29] Rabbi Yitzchak Huberman on Parshas Ke Sisah

[30] Yesodei Ha'Daas Chapter 47

[31] Taanis 25; Benayahu on Berachos 32

[32] Alshich Ha'Kadosh

[33] Shearim Be'Tefilah, Ittur

[34] Rabbi Tzaddok Ha'Kohen

[35] Yoma 29a

[36] Kihelos Yaakov; Tefilah Be'tzibur

[37] Chayei Olam p. 42, Toldos Yaakov, in the name of R'Eliezer Menachem Man Shach

[38] Letters of Reb Noson of Breslav

[39] Sefas Emes, Tehilim 27,14

[40] Degel Machane Ephraim

[41] Yismach Lev from Meor Einayim

[42] Meor Ha'Chayim p. 70

[43] Mishnas rebbe Aharon

[44] Shabbos 31a

[45] Poras Yosef

[46] Midrash Pinchas

[47] Rabbi Ezriel Tauber, *Beyond Surival*, pp. 82-85

[48] Olas Tamid, Chapter 21

[49] Marpeh Lashon

[50] Rokeach 28

[51] Shaloh Maseches Tamid; Benayahu Succah 14

[52] Michtav M'Eliyahu, 101

[53] Shaar 5, chapter 1

[54] Ibid Shaar Ha'Kollel, Chapter 18

[55] Michtav Me'Eliyahu; *The Art of Jewish Prayer*, Rabbi Y. Kirzner

Preparing for Prayer

Maximizing our Time with the Creator

Would a general begin a battle without investing time and effort on a plan of attack?[1] Would a person set out for an audience with the king without formulating his requests? Would a minister ask for forgiveness for having sinned against the crown without first spending time constructing a proper defense?[2] Would a farmer till the soil without having prepared the ground by removing the stones?[3]

It is certainly worthwhile to maximize our prayer time with advance preparation, setting aside a few minutes to mentally prepare ourselves to stand before our Maker.[4]

The original *chassidim* would wait one hour before beginning their prayers.[5] They used this hour for preparation – pushing aside alien thoughts and filling themselves with the fear and love of Hashem.[6] Even Moshe prepared himself before his prayers.[7] He turned aside, walking five steps before approaching Hashem at the burning bush.

Preparing for prayer begins with the decision to get to *shul* early in the morning; allowing ourselves time to develop the proper mindset. It involves clearing our minds of extraneous thoughts and focusing on our upcoming audience with Hashem. And there are many things we can do, even before prayer begins, to ensure that our entreaties will meet with acceptance.

Designating a Set Place to Pray

"A person who designates a set place to pray - his enemies will fall before him, the G–d of Abraham will surely assist him, and when the person departs the world they will mourn him and say, 'Woe! Where is the humble one? Woe! Where is the pious one, disciple of Avraham? " *(Berachos 6,2)*

Shmuel *HaKatan*, righteous composer of the benediction against heretics, was acclaimed in this manner. *Rabbenu* Yona wonders: Why is an individual who merely *davens* in the same place every day praised so extravagantly? The person who designates a place to *daven* is clearly taking careful measures to ensure that his prayer will be well received. The thought process behind the deed is what makes this commitment so noteworthy.[8]

One should not change his seat unless absolutely necessary.[9] Many people who hold prominent seats in *shul* will find that their seat is taken by the time they arrive. The *Ben Ish Chai* associates choosing a set place with humility. If a person humbly designates an unobtrusive place, no one will take that place.[10] Elsewhere he suggests another connection to humility: If a man designates a seat in his youth or when he is still a struggling beginner, and stays with that seat throughout his lifetime, into maturity and wealth, that is a true indication that he is a humble man.[11]

The author of *Hanosen Imrei Shefer (Parshas Achrei Mos)* also points out a connection between praying in an established place and humility. The most practical reason for maintaining an established place of worship is to avoid unnecessary changes, which can disrupt concentration. Just as a person finds it difficult to fall asleep when he is in a strange bed, so does a person experience difficulties concentrating on his prayers when he is in a different environment. A person who drifts from *shul* to *shul* arrogantly demonstrates that he considers himself to be above this type of consideration; suggesting that his constantly changing environment has no effect on the quality of his prayers.[12]

Many people would visit the shul where R' Yosef Salant prayed, in order to observe his devotions. He prayed so intensely that when he said the blessings from the Shacharis prayer at home, he had to be very careful to contain his enthusiasm so he would not wake the family.

After his Rebbetzin died, his son would beg him to come to his house for Yom Tov. R' Yosef refused, explaining that he was used to davening in his designated shul in the manner in which he felt comfortable. "This is my Yom Tov enjoyment, and I don't want it any other way, I can't do without it." (Told by his son and cited in Otzros Ha'Tefilah, page 724)

Harav Mandel, the tzaddik of Bnei Brak, told of a remarkable occurrence. "I myself saw how a place where a person prays becomes holy and has the power of pulling a person to it. On the night of Shavuos and Hoshana Rabbah, the custom in our shul is to spend the night studying in the women's section of the Bais Knesses. I would go up there to give an address. Each time it would be crowded and I would have to shuffle from place to place until I found a suitable spot to stand and talk. Year after year, I would end up in the same spot. I began to wonder which woman davened at that place. I was told that for decades, a certain tzaddekes used to pray there regularly, and women would gather around to listen to her. They would pray together with her and cry profusely. It was then that I came to fully appreciate how great are the words of Chazal who tell us that a place in and of itself can have a profound effect." (Sota 45) (Harav Mandel)

When Rabbi Moshe Aharon Stern heard, in the name of the Chazon Ish, that the place where Torah is studied is permeated with holiness, he was determined to find a sanctified spot for his own prayers. He chose the shul of the Gra and the seat where R' Shmuel Paperman had davened. R' Shmuel used to pray with overwhelming emotion and copious tears. After he passed away, Rabbi Moshe Yehoshua Landau, another distinguished scholar, took to praying in his spot. After his death, R' Stern asked for the seat. He felt it was a great merit to pray in this spot which had soaked up so much sanctity, purity and devotion to Hashem. (Ha'Mashgiach Me'Kaminetz)

The Environment for Prayer

One may not pray in the presence of someone dressed immodestly, in a dangerous or in an unclean place, or in front of a picture, painting or mirror. All these distract us from our prayers.[13]

A natural setting is conducive to spontaneous prayer. Meditation is particularly effective in grassy fields and amid trees. It is as if every blade of grass and every growing thing unite with man in prayer.[14]

Because humility in prayer is so important, we are instructed to pray from a low place, as it says, "From the depths I called to Hashem." *(Tehillim 130:1)* The *Maharal* views this verse as a requirement to call out to Hashem from the depths of our heart. How is this accomplished? By infusing our essence with subservience to Hashem.[15] A person who achieves this level of submission in prayer is considered as if he had offered up the entire roster of sacrifices in the Holy Temple of old.

One Succos, R' Aryeh Levine brought an esrog and lulav to a group of Jewish men imprisoned by the British. He led the prayers and read the Torah portion for them. When he was finished he told the prisoners, "It was a great merit for me to pray with you. I am confident that your prayers will be well received, for it says, 'From the straits I called Hashem,' (Tehillim 118) and 'From the depths I called You, Hashem.'"(Tehillim 130) Such was the humility of the tzaddik of Yerushalayim. (Ish Tzadik Haya)

Davening among people who pray with devotion makes it easier to pray properly.[16] Contemplating a great man or woman reciting the holy words with enthusiasm can be a tremendous inspiration to *daven* with greater fervor.

> *To impress on his children how to pray with feeling, the Mashgiach of Kaminetz would send his children to watch R' Yaakov Rotman, the Chazan of Zichron Moshe. Reb Yaakov involved every fiber of his being in his prayers. The Mashgiach himself would often watch Rav Avrohom Eliyahu Myzes pray. He was known far and wide for his heart-rending supplications, which inspired his listeners with awe. He also used to observe the saintly Rav Leib Todrus daven, whose tears would spill from his eyes as he prayed.*

> *R' Shmuel Tzvi Kowalsky attributed his attainment in prayer to an "accident." He arrived at Ponovitch as a young boy, and chose a spot in the Bais Midrash next to a very impressive looking gentleman. He soon discovered that his neighbor was Rabbi Dessler, the Mashgiach. As he later commented, "Whoever sat next to Rabbi Dessler could only utter heartfelt prayers."*

> *Rabbi Kowalsky's son studied in the Belzer Cheder. His classroom overlooked the shul where his father davened Shacharis. His teachers would take the child to the window so he could observe the enthusiasm with which his father prayed on a daily basis, and learn to pray accordingly. (Ana Avda)*

Rabbi Yehoshua Leib Diskin would daven alone in a room next to the minyan, with the door ajar. One day his student R' Tzvi Michel Shapira stood at the opening, observing his Rebbe complete the Maariv prayer of Shabbos.

When Rabbi Tzvi Michel arrived home for kiddush he told his family, "Before we welcome the heavenly angels, I want you to know that I have just observed an angel who lives among us. I observed my rebbe say 'Magen Avos,' and when he got to the words "Lefanav naavod be'yirah va'fachad' (Before Him we will serve with awe and dread) his face was as radiant as a torch and the vein in his forehead bulged the width of a finger. I was convulsed with trembling just observing such intense awe of the Creator. I am convinced that observing such a tangible manifestation of awe inspires fear of Hashem."

When his young son Ben Zion heard his father's statement, he became determined to acquire such fear. Every Friday night he stood at the opening to the Brisker Rav's room and observed his face redden and glow as he said the words with awe and trembling. These sessions had a tremendous impact on the five-year-old child. Many times during the course of the week, he could be overheard saying to himself with quivering excitement, "Lefanav na'avod be'yirah va'fachad'.

The regulars at the minyan got used to the way the child was always squeezing to the front. One of them asked R' Tzvi Michel if he was not concerned about the warning of our sages that observing a prince impairs the vision (Chagiga 16) because the Shechina rests upon him. "That is a fair price for *achieving fear of Hashem," was the father's reply.*

The child grew in fear, purity and devotion to Torah. When he was seven his father sent him to deliver mishloach manos to the tzaddik R' Uri Orenstein, who lay deathly ill. When the child entered the house the tzaddik opened his eyes and said to his son, "Who is this child whose face shines with pure fear of G–d?"

In those days, before the advent of antibiotics, infections led to serious illness. The child became seriously ill with an infection that took many lives. His parents prayed for a miracle. Friday night, at the exact time that the Brisker Rav started Magen Avos, the child called out from his burning stupor, "Lefanav na'avod be'yirah va'fachad!" He broke out in a sweat. The doctor declared that he had passed the crisis, and with Hashem's help he would recover. By the next week, he was again squeezing to the front of the regular daveners at the Brisker Rav's minyan.

The years passed, and the child became one of the most devoted disciples of the Brisker Rav. On the last Friday night of the Rav's life, he lay in bed unconscious. His students surrounded him. In the first row stood the senior disciples: the geonim R' Yosef Chayim Sonnenfeld, R' Yaakov Bornstein, R' Moshe Nachum Wallenstein and R' Tzvi Michel Shapira. Behind them stood the rest of the students.

Total silence dominated the full room, which was permeated by an awesome holiness. Suddenly a movement was detected. Ben Zion, now 26, pushed to the front, ignoring the wondering critical looks of the others. He had 21 years' of precedence backing him. He wanted to gaze at his rebbe's face - for what was possibly the last time.

The others viewed his attempt as unreasonable. The Rav's soul was preparing to rise to say his prayers before the heavenly court. Still, R' Ben Zion managed to squeeze up to the second row. But he could not budge the senior disciples, the Torah authorities who stood around their Rav. R' Ben Zion stood up on his toes to contemplate his Rebbe's face.

It was precisely the moment when the Brisker Rav would normally say the prayer 'Magen Avos.' His face began to flicker like a torch and the vein in his forehead bulged. Although his mouth was not moving, all those present could hear the Rav's voice saying 'Lefanav naavod b'yirah va'fachad'. They were all seized with trembling. (Ha'Saraf Me'Brisk)

The Ideal Time to Pray

The best time to recite *Shema* is at *vasikin*, just before sunrise, so one can begin *Shemoneh Esrei* exactly at sunrise.[17] R' Yonasan Eibshitz wrote in his commentary to Eicha that prayer said at sunrise is always accepted. If the Jewish people had davened at sunrise on the day of the Temple's destruction, the Temple would not have been destroyed.[18] There is no comparison between prayers said before sunrise and prayers said after sunrise.[19] A person who prays at sunrise will not be harmed that day.[20]

Reb Pinchas of Koretz wrote, "I like to daven at dawn, before the world is saturated with foolishness and inanities." (Midrash Pinchas chapter 46)

R' Yaakov Muzapi always davened vasikin. He would arrive an hour before davening started. No one ever managed to get there earlier then he did. On occasions when weakness prevented him from joining the vasikin minyan, he would daven at home. He did not want people to point a finger at him and say, "If R' Yaakov does not daven with the sunrise minyan, it is probably not worth the effort." (Maaseh Rav; Ari Alah Me'Bavel)

R' Ben Zion Yadler davened at sunrise into his old age. It made no difference if he slept six hours, four hours, or only two – he never missed the sunrise prayers. To insure that he always awakened in time, he tied a string from his basement to the Bais Midrash door. (Yalkut Amud Ha'Tefilah)

Those who strive to arrive on time benefit in this world and in the world to come.[21] A person who arrives promptly and is not in a hurry to leave the *Bais Midrash* will have enough time to enjoy his prayers, and is promised that his life will be prolonged.[22]

A person should rise at least half an hour before prayers to insure that he arrives on time.[23] He should resist the blandishments of the evil inclination: in the winter, "it's too cold;" in the summer, "you haven't slept enough." Strengthen your resolve and arise, for Hashem awaits us.

Our Sages have warned us that sleeping late removes a person from this world.[24] Those who arrive even a few minutes late are rushed before they start.[25] If a community has to labor to pull their *minyan* together each morning, it's a clear indication that there is little love in their hearts for Hashem.[26]

Rabbi Kalman of Doline would arise early to pray. He remarked, "When a merchant doesn't have the best merchandise to offer, he arrives at the marketplace early, before anyone else gets there." (A Touch of Wisdom, A Touch of Wit)

R' Naftali of Ropshitz once saw a young man running to shul after noon. The man put on his tallis and tefilin hurriedly. Before one could take a second glance, he had finished his prayers.

The rebbe called him over. "Let me tell you a story."

A certain man always had black bread and a dish of barley each day for breakfast. Whenever he came home from davening, his wife had the same meal ready for him.

One day he came home to find that there was nothing on the table. His wife called out to him from the adjoining room, "I haven't finished preparing your meal."

He waited patiently. One hour, two hours, three hours passed. He was really going to get a feast, he thought. Finally, after the three hours, his wife walked in - carrying a loaf of black bread and a dish of barley.

The man turned to his wife in astonishment. "After all that time, I was sure you were preparing something really special. If this was all you were going to cook, you could have served it early in the morning!"

"There are righteous sages who do not pray immediately," the rebbe explained. "They need time to meditate and compose themselves for prayer. Hashem wants their prayers and waits for them eagerly. This is the only justification for late prayers. But since your prayer is hurried anyway, you could have prayed early in the morning." (Ha'Osher She'Be'Tefilah)

In non-*chassidic* circles, late prayer is regarded as totally unacceptable under any circumstances. The Chofetz Chaim cited the following parable to explain why such prayer is to be avoided at all costs.

There was a villager who saved various bank notes over the years towards his daughter's dowry. When the time came to marry her off, the villager tried to shop locally - but the shop-keepers refused to accept his bank notes. So he traveled to the capital city and went straight to the treasury. As he waited in line, he saw many people turning in torn bank notes receiving new ones in exchange. Occasionally the clerk reprimanded them for allowing their bank notes to get so mangled. The villager looked with pride at his own bank notes, which were well preserved. Certainly he would have no trouble!

When his turn came, the villager proudly presented his bills. How surprised he was when after a cursory examination, the clerk returned them without a word. "You accepted old torn bills," the villager said in bewilderment. "What is wrong with my nice clean bills?"

"These bills expired and were removed from circulation long ago," the clerk explained. "They may be in good condition – but they are worthless. The others may be worn, but they are still in circulation."

Even if a person's prayers are said with only partial *kavana*, they are still accepted if they are offered on time. But once the gates of prayer are closed, all formal prayer is rejected.[27] In fact, not saying Shema on time is a transgression that cannot be rectified.[28]

Rabbi Moshe Aharon Stern would severely reprimand any boy who came late to davening. He would ask, "Do you think the Kohen Gadol would come late to his service in the Temple?"

He was deeply disturbed to see boys coming late, skipping portions of the prayer with the intention of making up everything later. He once asked a young man, "When was the last time you said everything in the proper order?" The boy thought for a moment, then replied, "Last Yom Kippur."

R' Moshe Aharon would wake his children at six o'clock so they would not be late for the 7:30 minyan. Once he got up in the middle of the night, very upset. When his wife asked what had happened, he told her that he had dreamt that he was late for minyan in the yeshiva.

R' Moshe Aharon once noted that R' Eliyahu Lapian seemed very tired for a few successive days. R' Elya explained that the Gra says that if a person sees his hair go white, he should view it as an indication that he will soon be standing before the Heavenly Court and he must begin his preparations.

"If they ask me if I fulfilled the Torah and mitzvos, presumably they will start with the first chapter of the Shulchan Aruch which deals with getting up in the morning. How humiliating it will be to be proven derelict in my duty at the very beginning of my life's review! To fulfill the injunction of rising with the strength of a lion to serve Hashem, I have been getting up several times during the night to be sure that I will not oversleep. That is why I am tired." (Ha'Mashgiach Me'Kaminetz)

R' Shlomo Zalmen Auerbach was once asked by a yeshiva boy what to do if he arrived late to shul. Should he say everything at top speed, or skip certain prayers as prescribed by the Shulchan Aruch so he could say select prayers with kavana?

R' Shlomo Zalmen was horrified by the question. "How can a yeshiva bochur ask such a question?" he exclaimed.

The boy hastened to excuse himself. "I was just wondering, in case it happens…"

But R' Shlomo Zalmen, aghast, repeated again, "How can a yeshiva boy ask this type of question?"[29]

There are certain times that are considered ideal for special requests:[30]

- Midnight.[31]

- When the morning star appears.[32]

- Before daybreak. The new day is dependent on the revelation of the special reserved light of creation. If a person prays at the moment this light is revealed, his request will be answered.[33]

- Any time one prays with a large number of Jews. A multitude's prayer is always heard.[34]

- During the silent *Shemoneh Esrei* – at the appropriate *berachah* for the specific request; at *Shomeah Tefilah*; and at the end of the *Amidah* prayer.[35]

- During *Nefilas Apayim*, when falling on one's face in prayer.[36]

- When the *Sefer Torah* is removed from the ark, the gates of heavenly compassion are opened.[37]

• The prayer of *Mincha* is considered an *es ratzon*, an opportune moment.

• From *Elul* through *Yom Kippur*, Hashem is especially attentive to our prayers.[38]

• During the *Ten Days of Repentance,* Hashem is on twenty-four-hour call.[39]

• When the *Kohanim* are blessing the people, the upper and lower worlds are blessed.

• On Monday and Thursday, Hashem carefully attends to our prayers.[40]

• At a *bris*, the crying of the infant raises all prayers.[41]

Arriving in Shul First

If people appreciated the significance of being first in *shul*, they would fight with one another for this privilege.[42] The reward for this cannot be measured.[43] Arriving in shul first guarantees long life;[44] the earlier arrival is called "friend" by the heavenly hosts,[44] and is considered righteous by the *Shechinah*.[46] The reward for arriving early may be greater than the reward for performing the *mitzvah* itself.[47] This is one of the easiest *mitzvos* for which one receives such a superlative reward.[48]

A king sent a message to the citizens of a certain city, informing them that he would be arriving on a certain day at a certain place. Everyone was still busy preparing when the appointed day arrived. Only one person hurried to the appointed place.

When the king arrived he found that one person waiting. "Where are the others?" the king asked.

"They will be here soon," the man explained.

The king was satisfied. He sat down to talk with the only man present. In the course of the conversation he grew to appreciate the man's fine qualities. As the others eventually arrived, the king was placated, and they were all sent home in peace.

What if no one had been there to receive the king and offer reassurances that the others would be coming soon? The king would have been very angry.[49] The presence of a single individual made it seem as if the others were present as well.

The *Shechinah* connects with the early arrival in *shul*, elevating that person to the level of *tzaddik*. But what if no one was there at all? As the verse says *(Yeshaya 3,2)*, "Why have I come and there is no man?"[50]

At the very least, a person should make the effort to be among the first ten arriving in *shul*.[51] The earlier one arrives, the closer one is to the source of holiness. The *Reishis Chochmah* knew people who would fast if they were not among the first ten to arrive in *shul*. He recommends that a person should penalize himself for coming late.[52] One who really wants to pray as he ought to will make the effort to be in *shul* early.[53]

Even if another one hundred individuals join the congregation, the first ten get the reward of them all.[54]

R' Yosef Chaim of Baghdad explains the arithmetic by comparing the value of precious stones. A diamond of one carat is worth 100 dinarim. But a ten carat diamond is worth far more than one thousand dinarim. Such a large diamond would be worth at least ten thousand dinarim - that is, one thousand for each carat.

Each of the first ten to arrive are considered like ten. They are the equivalent of the larger, rarer stones. Together they equal 100. They therefore receive a reward equal to the one hundred arriving after them. (Ben Yehoyada on Berachos 47)

R' Yehuda Tzedaka pointed out that when a person arrives in *shul* on time, he is given a reward for each step he takes towards his destination and back. If he arrives late, his reward begins from the moment he starts praying.

R' Yehudah was careful to always begin davening or learning immediately upon arrival in shul, so it was clear that his trek was strictly for spiritual purposes.

Once R' Yehuda met a rosh yeshiva who mentioned that during the summer his yeshiva relies on a leniency of the Gra, to enable the boys to pray later. R' Yehuda's face crumpled in anguish. "Is this the way a holy yeshiva should conduct itself? Perhaps it is acceptable to rely on a leniency in an emergency – but to do so on a regular basis for a group of Torah students? How is that possible?" he exclaimed.

He would often point out that the power of the yetzer hara is so great that it blinds our eyes. People cannot distinguish between what is important and what is insignificant. A person takes special care to purchase an expensive esrog which is kosher according to all opinions. But when it comes to the precious scriptural mitzvah of Krias Shema, people rely on all types of leniencies. Is this mitzvah any less important than that of the esrog and lulav?

Early one morning, at a large gathering for the mitzvah of blessing the sun, R' Yehuda commented sorrowfully, "Even mitzvos require mazal. The mitzvah of blessing the sun is of rabbinical origin, yet look how many people get up early to say it, perhaps because it is said only once every 28 years. The mitzvah of Krias Shema is scriptural, it can be said every day, and ideally it should be said at sunrise. Yet very few seize this mitzvah." (Ve'Zos Le'Yehuda)

Avoiding Distractions

Fortunate is the person who rises and prays before doing anything else, except for the study of Torah or saying *Tehillim*. When a person awakes in the morning, he is ready for a fresh start, as if he were born anew. If he is careful to keep his mind pure, without sullying his intellect with inappropriate or unnecessary thoughts, his prayers will be answered.[55]

R' Avraham of Koritz was very careful never to speak before Shacharis. One morning on his way to shul, he met a gentile who held a piece of gold in his hand. The gentile had found the gold and he offered it to R' Avraham at a low price.

Without speaking, R' Avraham signaled him to come to his home after davening to complete the deal. But the gentile would not wait. He went to another Jew and sold him the gold. That Jew became very wealthy.

That same night, R' Avraham dreamed of his father, R' Pinchas of Sokolow. In the dream, R' Pinchas told his son that Heaven had noted his refusal of great wealth because of his scrupulousness in not speaking before davening and had decided to grant him a son whose light would shine like gold throughout the world.

And indeed, a son was born to R' Avraham. He became R' Pinchas of Koritz, who illuminated his people with the light of his holiness and his Torah.

The Mishnah Berurah cites a similar story about R' Zalmen Mirels, who rejoiced at the opportunity to show his devotion to his prayers by not engaging in a potentially lucrative deal before his prayers.

R' Shmuel Paperman would not utter a sound before davening. He once met someone who had stopped to read the headlines of a newspaper on his way to shul. He reprimanded him, "How is it possible to get involved in something else when you are on the way to talk with the King?" (Sippurim Yerushalayim)

Talking unnecessarily before prayer will give rise to distractions during our devotions. Our minds will not be able to channel our thoughts into the words of prayer.[56]

The *Ben Ish Chai* is specific, "Ideally, try not to speak, listen or think about anything prior to *tefilah*.[57] Don't begin your day by discussing your business affairs. Before praying, don't discuss the daily news, for all this will distract you from your prayers. If you are feeling sad or troubled, change your focus before praying."[58]

When R' Shmuel Aharon Yudelevitz was asked a question on halacha before prayers, he refused to answer. "We are about to daven and I may not focus on anything but the prayers, for it is forbidden to begin praying after a judgment or involvement in the study of halacha so as not to be distracted during prayers." (Shulchan Aruch 93,3)

After completing his prayers, he told the questioners, "How perceptive are the words of our Sages, for despite my best intentions I formulated an answer to your question during my prayers." (Meilo shel Shmuel)

R' Yehuda Halevi notes that a person who is immersed in worldly concerns will have a hard time achieving *kavanah* in prayer. He describes how a chassid prepares for prayer: He curbs his pride, anger, and physical desires. He curbs his powers of imagination, reasoning, thought, memory, as well as his worldly longing. Only then is he ready to begin.[59]

Not Eating Before Prayers

One should not eat or drink before praying. Drinking coffee or tea is permissible, if this will enable the individual to concentrate better on prayers. Opinions vary as to whether milk or sugar may be added. One may eat or drink before praying if his health requires it.[60]

The *Gemara* informs us, in the name of R' Eliezer son of Yaakov, "Whoever eats and drinks and then prays, Hashem says, 'After he swells with pride he takes upon himself the yoke of Heaven?" *(Berachos 10)* What is the connection between pride and eating? A person should pray first to indicate that he has neither food nor drink nor money until he turns to Hashem to request them.

> The king had a loyal servant whom he supported. At the beginning of the year he gave him enough money to last throughout the year. Each morning before he went out to buy his daily supplies, the servant would go to the palace and stand in the courtyard for a few minutes. He would then go to the market and make his purchases. A friend asked him why he troubled to stop at the palace. The man explained that because he had only to reach in his pocket and help himself to cash, he could easily forget that the money didn't really belong to him. His visit to the palace was to remind him that the king was supporting him.

A person needs to visit the courtyard of the king, the *shul,* three times daily, to be reminded that Hashem is the source of his money. A person who eats before his visit to the king arrogantly ignores Hashem's role in his support.[61]

The prohibition is derived from the verse, "You shall not eat on the blood – *lo sochlu al ha'dam.*" *(Vayikra 19,26)* Before praying, man is merely flesh and blood. After praying, he is transformed into *Adam*, a combination of the letter *aleph*, which represents the Master of the world, and *dam*, which means blood. We are instructed not to eat before we've added the *aleph* to the *dam,* by *davening.*[62]

Getting Dressed for Prayer

Preparing oneself for prayer includes dressing with the proper decorum. One should wear the type of clothing that people wear when they meet with a prominent person. If one usually wears a hat when going out, he should wear one when praying as well. Even when one prays at home, his attire should be appropriate.[63] These preparations impress upon us the significance of standing in prayer before the King of the universe.

The Steipler once noticed a yeshiva boy praying without a hat and jacket. After prayers he went over to him and told him that he must always wear a hat and jacket for prayers, as it says, "Prepare to greet the G–d of Israel (Amos 4)."

In the last days of his life, R' Yechezkel Levenstein grieved at his inability to daven with proper kavana. He insisted on wearing his hat and frock for prayers even as his strength ebbed. One of his students who visited him the day before his death was informed that the Mashgiach had not had anything to drink that day. The student took some water into his rebbe and said that it was vital that he drink some. It seemed to the young man that the Mashgiach agreed, and yet when he raised

*the cup of water the Mashgiach did not react. Then the talmid
realized that he was not wearing his hat. Once he placed the
hat on R' Yechezkel's head, the Mashgiach recited the beracha
and drank the entire cup of water.*

The Importance of Attitude

Perhaps the most important prerequisite for prayer is an
earnest desire to pray with devotion.[64] Our Sages have said that
prayer is grounded in the heavenly spheres. One cannot reach
heavenly goals without a ladder. A person who circles the ladder,
and even occasionally longingly contemplates it, will get
nowhere. He must begin to actually ascend the ladder, rung by
rung.

We must apply ourselves to begin our ascent. Otherwise, we
may still be circling the base of the ladder into our old age. We
should not be disheartened at the enormity of the project, for we
are all capable of reaching this goal. Adam was a sublime creature,
the handiwork of Hashem. All the remarkable aspects of Adam's
greatness have been bequeathed to his descendents. Even after
Adam sinned, we can still access Adam's former greatness during
spiritually uplifting moments. We can use this power to scale the
heights of spirituality.[65]

Our Sages have informed us that nothing stands in the way of
a strong desire. "In a way that a person desires to go he is led."
(Macos 10) "Whoever comes to be purified is aided." *(Yoma 38)* If
man demonstrates his aspiration to achieve his goals, Hashem will

help him.[66]

> R' Chaim Todros Hershler was a well-known figure in
> Jerusalem's Yishuv Ha'Yashan. When he grew old, he was
> afflicted with an illness that affected his sense of balance,
> making it dangerous for him to remain erect. Despite his
> infirmity, he insisted on standing during Shemoneh Esrei.
> Afraid that he might fall and injure himself, his family plead-
> ed with him to follow the lenient opinion that permitted sitting
> in extenuating circumstances, but he adamantly refused. Sure
> enough, he once fell during his prayer, but fortunately he
> wasn't hurt. The family members again urged him to sit dur-
> ing Shemoneh Esrei. Rav Chaim responded, "I wrote a special
> prayer which I say before beginning Shemoneh Esrei, asking to
> be able to stand as the law requires. Today I did not say this
> prayer, and that is why I fell." (Ha'Mashgiach Me'Kaminetz)

Cultivating the right attitude is an indispensable prerequisite
for prayer. One should seriously reflect on the fact that he is about
to address Hashem directly, and should carefully choose both the
words and the themes he intends to contemplate. One should
keep in mind what he seeks to accomplish, then concentrate on
the words he utters before Hashem.[67]

Before prayer, one should pluck from his heart his yearning for
the mundane pleasures of this world.[67] Once we are convinced
that only spiritual goals are worth the effort, we are ready to begin.

Spiritual Reckoning

The *Chidushei Harim* suggests that before praying, everyone should take a few moments for a spiritual reckoning. Ponder on how good Hashem is to you, and how little you do in return. Feel indebted to Hashem for enabling you to become intimate with Him through prayer.[69]

In the preliminary prayer of the *siddur Yeshuas Yisrael*, it states, "Who am I that I should merit praying to the formidable and majestic G–d? I am a sinner who has angered the Great Name with my evil deeds. I am merely flesh and blood, ashes and dust, and I am unworthy of uttering His exalted and awesome name."

Our very insignificance makes it difficult for us to continue. It is at this point that we should remind ourselves, "Prayer is a *mitzvah* that we have been commanded to fulfill with enthusiasm and joy." Once we sense this joy surging within us, we are ready to pray.[70]

The *Sefer Ramasayim Tzofim* uses this concept to reconcile two contradictory verses in *Tehillim*. Dovid Hamelech first advises us to serve Hashem with fear[71] and elsewhere advises us to serve Him with joy.[72] The first verse refers to the necessary emotional groundwork prior to prayer; the second to our sentiments during prayer.[73]

A person who is not delighted at the chance to communicate with Hashem does not comprehend the sum and substance of the gift of prayer. He is like a person who finds a treasure of gold coins and counts his newfound riches with tears of sadness. Clearly, he has no understanding of the value of what he has discovered.[74]

The author of *Degel Machane Ephraim* writes that strengthening our faith and trust is the basis of all worship. The man of faith recognizes that Hashem constantly renews both the universe and man and naturally wants to sing His praises.[75]

Prior to the Days of Awe the Baal Shem Tov asked his disciple, Rabbi Dovid Farkas, to prepare to lead the congregation in prayers. Rabbi Dovid stayed in the synagogue day and night, sanctifying himself with numerous acts of piety. He studied the meanings of the words, resolutely preparing for this divine duty.

When Rosh Hashanah arrived, Rabbi Dovid walked to the front to begin the prayers. When the Baal Shem Tov saw him, he began to berate him relentlessly, "You vacuous one, do you really believe that you can represent this congregation? What impudence to presume that you have the ability to lead those assembled here! You are overflowing with sins. You have the impertinence to act as an advocate for this holy convocation, before their Father in Heaven, on this holy day?"

Reb Dovid was sorely distressed to receive such a tongue-lashing. In his heart he bewailed the sins which had caused his teacher to reprimand him so mercilessly. Waves of remorse washed over him. A hunger to repent surged within him, so great that it was hard to contain. The tears overflowed and tumbled down his cheeks. He sorrowfully beseeched Hashem to forgive him.

The Baal Shem Tov motioned for him to start. The tears

continued to flow as R' Dovid's prayers poured from the bottom of his heart.

After the prayers were completed, R' Dovid fearfully approached the Baal Shem Tov to ask him to reveal his sin. The Baal Shem Tov responded, "Reb Dovid, my son, you did nothing wrong. I wanted only to ensure that your heart was humbled before you began to lead the prayers, so your devotions would not be defiled by haughty thoughts." (Shivchei Besht, page 62)

Ahavas Yisrael as a Preparation for Prayer

If you are not at peace with the world, your prayer will not be heard.[76] The *Ari Ha'Kadosh* strongly recommended consciously feeling love of our fellow Jews prior to beginning our daily prayers.[77]

We must fill our hearts with compassion, forgiving anyone who has hurt us before we start to pray. We should make an effort to judge people favorably, and remove hate, jealousy and the desire for honor from our hearts. How can we appear before G–d with a garment soiled with the taint of evil intentions?[78]

Every soul contains within itself all other souls. Hatred of a fellow Jew causes a division within the soul, leaving a stain. Only the prayers of a wholesome soul that is at peace with all other souls are welcome.[79]

As a result of heartfelt *ahavas Yisrael*, G–d fulfills the requests made in the prayers. Before prayer, the *Baal Ha'Tanya* recommended that we recite, "I accept upon myself the responsibility to fulfill the positive commandment, 'Love your fellow as yourself.'" The feelings of love of our fellow Jew will thereby emerge from the realm of thought into the world of action.[80]

In his introductory prayer, R' Elimelech of Lizhensk included a request that Hashem should help us overcome envy of others and rid ourselves of hatred, so we see only the virtues of others.

Before the section dealing with the sacrifice of Yitzchak, one should say, "I undertake to love each Jew as I love my own soul. I will not speak *lashon hara*, hurt my friend, or hate my neighbor in my heart. I will rebuke my friend but I will not take revenge."[81]

Before leaving to daven, R' Moshe Kliers of Teveriya would serve his wife coffee to fulfill the requirement of demonstrating love for one's fellow Jew.

R' Moshe Shimon Weintraub, Mashgiach of Heichal Ha'Torah, studied in the Chevron Yeshiva. It was his custom to call the hospital regularly to ask if there was a need to pray on anyone's behalf. (Shem Olam)

Charity as an Aid to Prayer

Performing a *mitzvah* before *davening* is like planting a seed.

The sprouting of our spiritual seed will improve the quality of our prayers.[82] Just as spices bring out the real flavor in food, so charity seasons our prayers.[83]

The gates of Heaven are thrown open when a person performs a *mitzvah*. Rabbi Eliezer would give charity before *davening* to open the gates of Heaven.[84] The charity one gives before praying serves as an advocate between man and his Father in Heaven, preparing the way for Hashem to accept one's prayers favorably.[85]

The Tzalka Rav would break off a portion of his meager bread in the concentration camp and give it to a fellow prisoner to fulfill the obligation of giving charity before prayer. (The Tzedaka Treasury, pages 262-263)

Whoever is charitable is assured that his prayers are answered.[86] When we are generous we arouse Hashem's Divine attribute of mercy. Appropriately, we give charity before approaching Hashem, allowing Him to rest His mercy on us.[87]

Before reciting his prayers, R' Aharon of Karlin would give charity to the poor of the Land of Israel in a pushka set aside for this purpose. He explained that one's prayers anywhere in the world will be channeled through the Land of Israel by giving tzedakah to its poor, and the tefilah will be much more effective. (Tiferes Banim 2,104)

Good Character Facilitates Davening

Rabbi Elye Lapian writes that prayerful devotion requires

three things: a great deal of practice, much Torah wisdom (so one's thoughts are immersed in Torah study only), and good character. Regarding the latter, one who does not possess a refined character will find that anger and resentment prevent him from praying properly, plaguing him in the midst of his prayer.[88]

If a person has to visit a dangerous place, he should take reliable people along with him for protection. Similarly, if good deeds precede our sincere prayer, our prayer will be well received.[89] Just as we would seek an immaculate vessel to hold a gift for the king, so must we be sure that our prayer is proffered in a pure vessel, an untainted mouth.[90]

A group of individuals who had rebelled against the king later regretted their deed. They were too ashamed to ask the king for a pardon. Instead, they sought a man who would approach the king on their behalf. They chose someone who frequented the palace to be their representative. They knew that only someone who was totally uninvolved in the rebellion could defend their actions to the king.

There is no righteous person who has not sinned with one of his limbs. When he later regrets his deeds, he seeks to confess his sin. The mouth is the organ that frequents the king's palace. It prays and sings Hashem's praises. The mouth acts as the representative for our other limbs, provided that we have not used it to sin. If we have spoken *lashon hara*, then our lips and tongue have also rebelled against the king. Who then will be able to come before the king and plead for the other limbs? The one thing that can save us when all else is lost is a pure mouth.[91]

The *metzorah*, whose mouth has been sullied with *lashon hara*, must call out his affliction to others so they can pray on his behalf – for his own prayers are valueless.[92]

"There are a number of accusers whose task is to seize any bad word or foul word that a person brings forward from his mouth. When he later brings forward holy words, woe to them! Woe to their lives! Woe to them in this world and woe to them in the world to come! The accusers, these defiled spiritual beings, take those defiled words and . . . they defile the holy words, so they can bring no merit to him." *(Zohar)*

Our evil words create a whole army of soldiers who help the *yetzer hara* block our attempts at prayer. When we refrain from sharing a bit of gossip, or uttering something harmful, we kill one and sometimes many, of these soldiers.[93]

When someone consistently uses his power of speech in a positive way, the spiritual power of his prayer is infinitely enhanced and endowed with an exalted spiritual light.

There was once a son who went on a long journey. The father yearned to hear from his son. He hungered for some sign that all was well. Had his son forgotten the father who loved him?

All the time that he was away, the son was writing letters full of longing to his father. He asked for advice and support and received no answer. The son wondered why his father was ignoring his letters.

Words of prayer uttered by a person who lies and speaks

lashon hara are transported to the realm of evil and never reach Hashem. Even the best prayers will not rise to heaven if a person has not repented for the lashon hara he has spoken.[96] No wonder our prayers are not always answered! Meanwhile, Hashem wonders why no one turns to Him.[97]

Torah as an Aid to Prayer

The study of Torah brings man close to Hashem. A person who studies before praying finds it easier to concentrate and address Hashem.[98]

The *Chazon Ish* writes that toiling in the study of Torah invigorates prayer and conversely, prayer aids in the study of Torah.[99]

> *When approached by a childless couple to daven on their behalf, the Chofetz Chaim eventually agreed, provided that they in turn agreed that the child would devote himself to the service of Hashem. He also insisted that they not tell anyone of his promise, for, "If the word gets out, then I will have to flee and hide for I will not have any time to learn Torah."*

> *That year the couple had a boy. Only after the Chofetz Chaim's death did they reveal the miracle surrounding their son's birth. (Dugma Mi'Sichos Avi)*

> *R' Avraham Trop, who later became a rosh yeshiva of Karlin in America, would tell his own miracle story involving the Chofetz Chaim. When he was studying in the Chofetz Chaim's yeshiva, he became seriously ill. When his friends*

saw he was close to death, they ran to the Chofetz Chaim, crying, "Avraham Trop is dying." The Chofetz Chaim told them to hurry back and whisper in his ears that if he accepted upon himself to teach Jewish children Torah, he would recover.

The boys hastened to their friend's bedside, only to find that he was already unconscious. No longer able to follow the Chofetz Chaim's recommendations, they raced back to their Rebbe to inform him that the situation had worsened. The Chofetz Chaim rushed back with them and ordered everyone out of the sick room. The boys put their ears to the door and their eyes to the keyhole. They observed the Chofetz Chaim walk to the wall and start to call out the names of the father and grandfathers of the dying boy. He beseeched these great souls to hurry to the Heavenly Throne and announce that their descendant, Avraham, was accepting upon himself to devote his life to teaching Torah to Jewish children.

He then left the room. A short time later, Rav Trop's friends noted that he was showing signs of improvement. After a while he was back to his regular routine. (Sheal Avicha Ve'Yagedcha)

1 Shearim Be'Tefilah

2 Nefutzos Yisrael by the Chofetz Chaim

3 Daliyos Yechezkel 2,76

4 Hilchos Tefilah 4,16

5 Berachos 30

6 Mesilas Yesharim Chapter 17

7 Tefilas Channah

8 See Sifasei Renanos on a set place of prayer

9 Orchos Yosher

10 Benayahu, Berachos 6

11 Ben Yehoyada, Berachos 6

12 Zelach; Me'Am Loez, Bereishis 386

13 Mishnah Berurah 10

14 Rebbe Nachman

15 Nesivos Olam, Nesiv Ha'Avodah

16 Shaloh Ha'kadosh, Maseches Tamid

17 Mishnah Berurah 58,1

18 Orchos Yosher

19 Last will and testament of the Baal Shem Tov

20 Berachos page 9 see Tosfos

21 Shabbos 127

22 Olelos Ephraim part 4, page 2, 503; Shaloh Ha'Kadosh Ner Mitzvah

23 Mishnah Berurah 1,169

24 Avos, 3,9

25 Shearim Be'Tefilah

26 Meiri, Berachos 6

27 Siach Yisrael, page 307

28 Chagigah 9; Berachos 63

29 Rabbi Shlomo Zalmen Auerbach

30 Es Ratzon in Otzros Yerushalayim

31 Shaloh Ha'Kadosh in the name of the Idra

[32] Zohar page 45

[33] Imrei Pinchas, Parshas Shemos

[34] Rambam, Hilchos Tefilah, chapter 8, Halacha 10

[35] Tikunei Zohar, Tikun 38

[36] Zohar, page 200

[37] Zohar, page 206

[38] Shaar Ruach Ha'Kadosh, page 50

[39] Rosh Hashanah 18

[40] Ramah Siman 134,1

[41] as advised by the Greidittzer Tzadik

[42] Meam Loez, Devarim, page 533

[43] Yesod Ve'Shoresh Ha'Avodah 2,7

[44] Menoras Ha'Maor 3,3; Olelos Ephrayim 4,2,503; Shaloh Ner Mitzvah; Reishis Chchmah, Tozaos Chaim 38

[45] Zohar, Pikudei page 203

[46] Reishis Chochmah, Tozaos Chaim Letter mem

[47] Daas Torah Parshas Vayeirah

[48] Yaalozu Chassidim by the author of the Peleh Yoetz

[49] Zohar, Parshas Terumah

[50] Ibid as cited in Yesod Ve'Shoresh Ha'Avoda 2,87

[51] Berachos 47; See Menoras Ha'Maor 3,3

[52] Tozaos Chaim letter mem

[53] Sichos R' Nosson Wachtfogel

[54] Berachos 47

[55] Or Haganuz Parshas Bo

[56] Reishis Chochmah, Shaar Ha'Kedusha; Yesod Ve'Shoresh Ha'Avodah 5,1; Imrei Pinchas 3:4; Kaf Ha'Chaim 11:18

[57] Olas Tamid, Chapter 13

[58] Beniyahu on Berachos 31

[59] Kuzari 1,60

[60] Shulchan Aruch Orach Chaim 89,3; Mishnah Berurah 22

[61] Ben Yehoyada

[62] Magid of Mezhritch

[63] Shulchan Aruch, Orach Chaim 91; Mishnah Berurah 12

[64] Yesod Ve'Shoresh Ha'Avodah, Shaar 5,chapter 1

[65] Shearim Be'Tefilah, Chilui

[66] Alei Shur Part One

[67] Rokeach Introduction

[68] Ramah, Orach Chayim 98,l

[69] Toldos Yaakov Yosef, Ki Savoh

[70] Maayan Ha'Nitzchi, page 92

[71] Tehillim 2,11

[72] Tehillim 100,2

[73] Ramasayim Tzofim 51

[74] Shearim Be'Tefilah, Rina

[75] Degel Machane Efraim, pages 234-235

[76] Sefer Ha'Midos

[77] Pri Etz Chaim, Shaar Olam Ha'Asiya chapter 1, Gate 3; Shaar Ha'Kavanos of R'Chaim Vital chapter 2

[78] Yaaros Devash, Derush 5

[79] Siddur of the Alter Rebbe page 22

[90] see Sanhedrin 65a; Bava Metziah 90; Siddur of the Alter Rebbe

[81] Olas Tamid Chapter 14

[82] Daas Chochmah U'Mussar Part 2

[83] Kav Ha'Yashar 58

[84] Bava Basra 10; Shearim Be'Tefilah, Chilui

[85] Meiri on Bava Basra 10

[86] Midrash Shochar Tov 65

[87] Ollelos Ephraim 502

[88] Lev Eliyahu pages 59-60

[89] Agudas Ezov

90 Sefer Ha'Midos

91 Yitav Lev, Parshas Metzorah

92 Shemiras Ha'Lashon

93 Leket Reshimos relating to the Bais Midrash of R' Noson Wachtfogel, Menucha U'Kedusha chapter 35

94 Magid Mi'Lublin as cited in Shaarei Armon

95 Marpeh Lashon

96 Tehillim 42:10-11

97 Yeshayah 50:2

98 Rabbi Menachem de Lunzano

99 Kovetz Igros 1,2

Standing Before Hashem

The Approach to Prayer

Prayers should be said with awe and humility; not with frivolity or anger. One should pray with a feeling of happiness, brought on by the knowledge of Hashem's historic kindness to Israel and His mercy to all creatures.[1] The *Gemara* advises us to lower our eyes and raise our hearts.[2] Our eyes are lowered in contemplation of our physical inferiority; our hearts are raised in contemplation of G–d's greatness.[3]

Sincere communication with Hashem is an intense experience. This is why prayer is considered an immense *avodah,* a labor. A person should put all his energy into his prayers. This is the deeper meaning of, "For Your sake we have been killed all day long."[4]

R' Shlomo Zalmen Auerbach's prayers would exhaust him. He used every bit of stamina he possessed to pray on behalf of others. Because his prayers drained him, he had to limit the amount of prayers said for each person. (HaMaor HaGadol)

Man should approach *tefillah* with a readiness to sacrifice his life for Hashem's sake. The bond created by intense prayer can actually jeopardize one's existence. Indeed, there were many *tzaddikim* who would lose consciousness during the course of their prayers. According to the Baal Shem Tov, it is truly a great act of charity that Hashem endows man with the strength to continue his *tefillos*.[5]

R' Uri of Strelisk would bid farewell to his family before leaving for shul each morning, for fear that the intensity of bonding to Hashem might be irreversible.

The Yismach Moshe would daven at great length in his private room, pouring out his heart to his Creator. He often did not finish davening Shacharis until the late afternoon. Once, R' Moshe's great-grandson noticed that he had not heard any noise from his grandfather's room for some time. He opened the door and was shocked to see R' Moshe lying unconscious on the floor. R' Yoel ran to his great grandfather and checked his pulse. When he saw there was none he immediately called the doctor. Before the doctor arrived, R' Moshe had regained consciousness. He immediately cried out the last word of Shema Yisrael – "Echad."

Praying with Awe

Prayer should infuse us with a powerful awareness of Hashem's grandeur and awe of His majesty. The person who succeeds in internalizing this concept will instinctively cover his face in an act of humility.[6] Falling on our faces in the course of our prayers reflects our fear of the *Shechinah*. It is a visible manifestation of total subjugation of body and senses.[7]

The heavenly hosts quiver and tremble and fall on their faces when they have the opportunity to utter Hashem's name. How appalling it is that man can say Hashem's name with no *kavanah* and with *lese majesty*, G–d forbid![8]

One of his students wrote that when R' Elchonon Wasserman put on his tefillin and said the beracha, they all felt the same awe and trembling as they did on Rosh Hashanah at the blessing on the blowing of the shofar. (Or Elchonon)

Many people testified that when the Chazon Ish davened he visibly trembled. (Maaseh Ish)

When the Skulener Rebbe davened, his intense awe was apparent to all. When he was hospitalized, his heart monitor normally registered about 80 beats a minute. Each time he said Hashem's name in a beracha or in his prayers, the heart monitor would register a quickened heartbeat at double his normal rate. Even though he was so weak that only his mouth moved, the monitor revealed the intensity of emotion in his heart. (Introduction to Noam Eliezer)

Humility and Prayer

The purpose of prayer is not to change the will of Hashem; it should be viewed as an act of submission to His will.[9] Only the prayers of the humble are accepted[10] because Hashem abhors an egotist. The *Chovos Halevavos* cites the ideal prayer of a righteous individual who thanks Hashem for the opportunity to praise Him, avowing his submission with his worshipful stance. He catalogues his wants only to emphasize his neediness and dependence on Hashem.[11]

Pride is the main stumbling block to prayer. The dominant thought of the arrogant, even as they pray, is that "their might and strength are responsible for their accomplishments." This interferes with their ability to acknowledge their indebtedness to Hashem and their dependence on Him.[12] In the midst of their prayers, they pretentiously intersperse plans to increase their glory and demean others.

Perhaps this is why the sacrifices of proud men are loathsome to Hashem.[13] The purpose of a sacrifice is to break a person's ego, so he is inspired to correct his evil deeds. As the wicked have no intention of repenting, their offering is rejected.[14]

The Hebrew word for ark, teiva, also means "word." When Hashem told Noach to enter the teiva, he was also instructing him to enter into the word. What word is this? According to R' Moshe of Kobrin, this means totally immersing oneself into each word of prayer. A chassid asked, "How can a human being possibly enter into a diminutive word?" Replied Rabbi Moshe, "I am not speaking to anyone who considers himself to be bigger than a word."

A chassid covered his head with a tallis and began swaying during the prayer "Nishmas kol chai." The Rebbe chided him,

"You should know that the yetzer hara can fit between one's head and one's tallis, too. He will knock you down because of your pride." (Kol Dodi Dofek, page 79)

Pride can be compared to the peel of a fruit. Man was originally pure, but as a result of his sins he acquired an external shell of arrogance and denial, convinced that he is responsible for all his accomplishments. When he *davens* with humility, he peels away the external layers of sin, so he can function as was intended – acknowledging Hashem's generosity.[15]

Kavanah can be compared to a key. Thieves don't often have keys, but they can open many locks by simply forcing them. A person who finds that he is not achieving *kavanah* must not despair. Instead, he should learn from the thief and break the lock. By filling himself with awe of Hashem's grandeur and breaking his heart with humbleness, he will be able to tear down the obstructions which separate him from his Father. Subduing the heart destroys all barriers.[16]

A group of sages were praying together with great devotion. It was revealed to them from Heaven that although their prayers were remarkable, it had been decreed that they be penalized for not crowning their prayers with humility. They were spared punishment because one member of their group had prayed in a humble manner. (Peleh Yoetz)

Our sages instituted bowing as part of prayer in order to inculcate humility and bear witness to our dependence on Hashem.[17] During the Temple period, the more prominent an individual, the more times he had to bow during the *Amidah* prayer.[18] A *Kohen Gadol* bowed at the beginning of each *beracha*, whereas the king would bow and not rise until the end of his prayers, as it says in *Melachim 1,8*, "Shlomo Hamelech completed his prayers... And he rose from before the altar of Hashem, having crouched on his knees." Because of the honor customarily showered on these individuals, it was necessary that they take tangible steps to ensure that humility penetrate into their very being.[19]

When we bow we look at the ground, which symbolizes the fact that our bodies will eventually lie in the earth. Then we rise, to indicate that our souls will ascend to Hashem.[20] We always straighten up from bowing when we get to Hashem's name, just as Hashem raises us from the dust, sustains and energizes us.[21]

> *When R' Chaikel of Amdur said the words "Beyado afkid ruchi - into His hand I submit my spirit," he fainted. When he regained consciousness he told the men standing around him the following parable: A king once commanded his subjects to bring all their valuables to him. One of those who came was an extremely destitute man who carried all of his belongings in one small kerchief. Seeing the vast wealth that others had brought the king, the poor man broke down in tears, embittered by the knowledge that he had so little to offer his sovereign. "When I saw the lofty service that the angels and Seraphim offer Hashem, I felt exactly like the destitute subject, because I could only offer my poor spirit." (Maasei Avoseinu)*

If man acknowledges that he is not in command and that Hashem controls everything, his prayer is accepted.[22] Humble requests, consciousness of one's unworthiness and cognizance of the greatness of Hashem are the three ingredients of successful prayer.[23] However, too much humility can serve to distance man from Hashem. Why is this so?

The evil inclination has many ways to keep a man from praying. One tactic is to try to convince him that he is unworthy of praying because of his many sins. We must always remember that a Jew is never rejected and that the *Shechinah* is present even when a person sins. As it says, "For I am Hashem residing with them in the midst of their impurity." *(Vayikra 16, 16)*[24]

We must seek the proper balance of humility. To counteract the evil inclination, man should focus on the loftiness of his soul until he is firmly convinced that his *tefillos* do make an impact.[25] Hashem, who can convert coal into diamonds, ensures that even lowly man can achieve spiritual greatness.[26] We have many good deeds to our credit and have brought much joy to Hashem.

> *Dovid Hamelech said, "Were you to lie within your boundaries, dove's feathers plated with silver..." (Tehillim 68,14) The Hebrew for boundaries, sifasaim, can also be translated as lips. Hashem hovers over our utterances in loving anticipation of our heartfelt words of Torah and prayer. This should stir us to our very depths and inspire us to a heightened service of Hashem. (Toldos Yaakov Yosef, page 172)*

Submissive Prayer

The *Shevet Sofer* suggests that we approach our prayers as a man who has no resources appeals to his Creator, knowing that only Hashem can help Him.[27] David *Hamelech* refers to himself throughout *Tehillim* as a poor and destitute man. Rav Yechezkel Levenstein writes that one should pray like a beggar standing at the door with outstretched palms. We must intensify our awareness that our existence is entirely dependent upon Hashem.[28]

When Esther falls at the feet of Achashverosh, crying and pleading with him to absolve Haman's decree, the Torah uses the term *nefillah*, falling. Esther was fully conscious of the fact that no other human being could annul this decree.

This type of prayer consists of utter nullification before Hashem. The one who prays is completely aware that only Hashem can help him, as the following story illustrates.

The month of Adar was nearly at an end, yet no rain had fallen. The people sent a message to Choni, asking him to pray for rain. He prayed, but no rain fell. He then drew a circle, stood within it, and exclaimed, "Sovereign of the Universe, Your children have turned to me because they believe my prayers are effective. I swear by Your great name that I will not move from here until You have mercy upon your children!"

It began to drizzle. His disciples said to him, "We hoped you would save us from death, but this rain looks as if it came down merely to release you from your oath." Choni then exclaimed, "It is not for this that I have prayed, but for rain to fill cisterns, ditches and caverns." The rain then began to come down with great force, every drop as big as the opening of a barrel, and the sages estimated that no drop was less than a pint.

His disciples then said to him, "Master, save us from death. It looks as if the rain has come down to destroy the world." He then turned to Hashem and said, "It is not for this that I have prayed, but for rain of benevolence, blessing and bounty." The rain then fell normally, until the Jews in Yerushalayim were compelled to seek shelter from it.

His disciples then said to him. "Master, in the same way as you have prayed for the rain to fall, pray for the rain to cease." He replied, "It is not appropriate to pray to be relieved of an excess of good. However, bring me a bull for a thanksgiving offering." They brought him a bull and he laid both hands upon it. He said, "Sovereign of the Universe, Your people Yisrael cannot endure an excess of good, nor an excess of punishment. When You were angry with them they could not endure it. When You showered upon them an excess of good they could not endure it. May it be Your will that the rain may cease and that there be relief for the world." Immediately the wind began to blow and the clouds scattered and the sun shone and the people went out into the fields and gathered the mushrooms that sprang up after rain.

After this incident, R' Shimon ben Shetach, the head of the Sanhedrin, sent a message to Choni: "Were it not that you are Choni, I would have placed you under a ban for tampering with rain. But what shall I do? You lord over the Omnipresent and He grants your desire, as a son who lords over his father

*and is granted his desire. You are like a child who says to his
father, 'Give me a hot bath or a cold shower. Give me nuts,
almonds, peaches and pomegranates,' and he gives them to
him. Of you Scripture says, 'Let your father and your mother
be glad, and let she who bore you rejoice.'" (Taanis 19a)*

Another requirement of submissive prayer is a profound
awareness of how desperately one needs that which he is
requesting. Yaavetz's prayer is the standard for a prayer of desper-
ation. He asked that Hashem bless him with an understanding of
Torah and grant him disciples who will study at his feet; he
requested that Hashem ensure that he not forget the Torah that he
had already mastered. Finally, he entreated Hashem to provide
him with friends to help him overcome his *yetzer hara*. He ended
his prayer by saying, "If You grant my request, then all will be
well; if not, I will die of anguish." Hashem immediately agreed to
his bold request, for Yaavetz was convinced that his life depend-
ed on it.[29]

David Hamelech writes, "I swear that I stilled and silenced my
soul, like a suckling child at his mother's side." *(Tehillim 131,2)* A
suckling infant is totally dependent on his mother. When the baby
cries in the middle of the night, his mother readily rises to feed
him, for if she does not get up to nurse her child, he will be overcome by hunger. When the child is older and persists in waking
her at night with his crying, she finds it more difficult to feel
compassion for her child and resents being woken. His capacity to
care for himself diminishes her altruistic capacities. It works the
same way with Hashem. When we rely totally on Hashem like a

newborn child on his mother, Hashem ensures that we lack nothing. If we rely on our own abilities, then Hashem steps out of the picture.

This explains why Hashem is quick to respond to the prayers of widows and orphans. They have no one else to turn to and are utterly dependent on Hashem. Hashem ensures that they lack nothing. A person who is convinced that there is no possible alternative for remedying his situation, and cries out to Hashem as if he were parentless and friendless, will arouse Hashem's compassion. He is certain to have his prayers answered.

David Hamelech, knowing the power of this type of prayer, purposely kept his troubles hidden from others.[30] He avoided confiding even in those who might help him, to retain his total dependence on Hashem.

On Yom Kippur the Kohen Gadol would pray that "the prayer of travelers should not enter before You." (Yoma 53b) It is highly enlightening that the Kohen Gadol's short prayer should include a request that Hashem not accept the prayers of the travelers who pray that it should not rain. (ibid Rashi)

The Jews living in Eretz Yisroel were always very dependent on rain. If rain was delayed the community would decree fasts and communal teshuvah so Hashem would relieve the drought. (Taanis 10-13) Yet, if a poor wayfarer sees rain clouds and begs Hashem to withhold the rain, for he has no coat and no one to care for him if he takes ill, Hashem might very well listen to his prayers. Because he has no one to rely on but on his Father in Heaven, his prayer from the heart is very effective. It can carry more weight then all the prayers and fasts of the community. This is why the Kohen Gadol took the time during the holiest day of the year, in the holiest place, to nullify the power of the traveler's prayer. (A Pure Fire, page 100)

As long as Moshe raised his hands upwards, the Jews could overpower the *Amalekim*.[31] The hands of Moshe did not wage war; but as long as the Jews looked Heavenward and subjugated their hearts to their Father in Heaven, they overcame their enemies. Elsewhere Moshe is commanded to place a serpent on a flagpost, so those who were bitten would see it and live. Does a pinioned snake cause death or life? Again, when the Jewish people looked upward, subduing their hearts to Heaven, Hashem helped them and they were cured.

The *Tiferes Yisrael* explains that if the Jews had simply prayed to be saved from the hands of *Amalek* or from snakes and scorpions, their prayer would have been ignored. It was granted because they subjugated their hearts to their Father in Heaven. This approach is important, not only for prayer but also for life. All our deeds have to be imbued with subservience towards Hashem.

Rabbeinu Yona points out that this is a huge, but not insurmountable, task. It must be mastered if our prayers are to have any value.

Prayer Should Be Joyful

Joy is a fundamental principle in Divine service.[32] Dovid

Hamelech used his harp to accompany his prayers to fill his heart with the joy of love of Hashem.[33] His joy waxed so strong within him that his lips moved of themselves and sang. When Dovid observed how the Jews made their donations towards the building of the *Bais Hamikdash* with joy, he prayed that this joyous spirit should remain with them and not depart.[34]

Engaging in a *mitzvah* engenders powerful forces which can be harnessed to lift up our hearts and minds in prayer. The *Ari* revealed to his disciple, R' Chaim Vital, that he was granted understanding and spiritual elevation only in the merit of his joy.[35]

Our sages placed *Pisukei DeZimra* at the beginning of our prayers to heighten our joy in the service of Hashem. We begin the main body of our prayers by praising and extolling our loving Father, and proclaiming that all events in nature and human life can be traced back to Him. This realization should be a fountain of happiness, watering the withered recesses of our soul.[36]

Joy that is associated with materialism is always mixed with sadness. There is always a possibility that the object will be lost or stolen, and there are others who possess more. But joy that is associated with spiritual meditations creates no barrier between the individual and Hashem. He can begin his prayers with a clear conscience and a light heart.[37]

As R' Yehuda Tzedaka prepared for davening, he would sing to himself the words, "Yisrael, prepare to meet your G–d." During his prayers his eyes never left his siddur. His face showed signs of intense concentration when in conversation with his Master, as well as great joy when singing the praises of his Creator. (VeZos LeYehuda)

There was once a pious man who stopped to pray Mincha in the forest. Because he was so engrossed in his prayers he did not see the king and his entourage stop to watch him. The king was fascinated by the aura of intense attachment that enveloped the man.

When the man had finished his prayers the king asked him what he had been saying. The man replied, "I prayed to my Creator that He provide me with all my needs. I made my requests for the future and thanked Him for the past."

"How often do you do this during the course of your life?" asked the king.

The man replied, "Three times daily."

When the king heard this, he remarked, "Every soldier desires to be a commander. The commander aspires to be a general, the general a minister and the minister a king. What is the greatest aspiration of the king? He dreams of his armies extending his territory.

"Yet it seemed to me that the joy and contentment on your face as you were praying was greater than mine when I receive the joyful news of victory. I don't believe that it is realistic to expect more than two or three such conquests during the course of my lifetime. It is hard to believe that you experience such joy three times a day!"

Such is the joy of a righteous man who overflows with inner contentment. His enjoyment of those moments of closeness with Hashem is so great that he forgets he is in a concrete building, for in reality he is riding in the chariot of the King. He is attached to his Creator and trusts in Him. He is secure in this world, and in the world to come his reward will give him pleasure beyond description.[38]

R' Hirsch of Riminov would sing his prayers joyously together with a choir and instrumentalists. Even the most depraved sinner would repent from the depths of his heart after hearing the Rebbe's prayers. (Shomer Emunim)

R' Evo said, "When you stand before Him in prayer, let your heart rejoice that you are praying to a G–d without parallel." *(Midrash Shochar Tov)* This is true joy – rejoicing that one has been privileged to serve the Blessed Master, who has no equal. The more a person is privileged to understand of the greatness of the Blessed One, the greater his heart rejoices within him.[39]

One morning R' Yechezkel Abramsky shared his thoughts about the prayer Baruch She'amar with a confidant. "When I said the words, 'And through the psalms of David Your servant we shall laud You, Hashem our G–d, with praises and songs. We shall exalt You, praise You, glorify You…' I stopped myself and asked if it is possible for us to properly exalt Hashem. I concluded that it refers to entrenching within our own hearts an understanding of Hashem's greatness and loftiness." (Pninei Rabenu Yechezkel)

"Take joy in serving Hashem with prayer," writes R' Chaim Volozhiner. We should reflect on whom we are praying to. We are praying to Hashem, who is unique in His greatness. There is no greater bliss than the knowledge that we are worthy of serving Hashem and thereby acquiring eternal life. Eternal life is not for a few decades, or for a thousand or even tens of thousands of years — it means for an eternity, beyond all time.[40]

The omnipotent and omniscient Creator chose us, insignificant creatures, to praise Him. How can this thought not suffuse us with joy? Reflect, too, on Hashem's generosity in granting us a reward for this service. Blessed is the son of man, who sustains the world with his prayers and delights the great and exalted King. What a privilege to stand before Him. What joy![41]

Our prayers fashion a crown for the King of the world. "How have I merited the privilege of presenting a crown to the King of the world?" a person should ask himself. "The King in His great compassion has enabled me to come close to Him. My only possible response to this honor is to serve Him with joy!"[42]

A person who clinches a business deal in which he earns a few thousand dollars is happy. If he had made tens of thousands of dollars on the same deal, he would have been still happier. If he were to earn these tens of thousands of dollars with only minimal effort, his heart would overflow with joy. Yet this type of accomplishment pales in significance when compared with attainments of the spirit. One hour of satisfaction in the world to come is greater than all the enjoyment in this world.

When a chassid asked the Baal HaTanya how to arouse a feeling of joy in his heart, the Baal HaTanya was genuinely surprised at the question. Just uttering the blessing, "Who has not made me a gentile" in the morning prayers should kindle great joy in one's heart, enough to last all day. Just remembering that you are a Jew is the perfect recipe for joy. (Marbitzei Torah MeOlam HaChassidus).

The Holy One Blessed be He stormed against the Jews because they did not serve Him with joy, as it says, "Because you did not serve the Lord your G-d with happiness and willingness of heart." *(Devarim 28,47)* Our relationship with Hashem is reciprocal. Hashem is our shadow: just as a shadow dances if we prance about, and droops if we sag, Hashem will reflect our behavior. If we cleave to Hashem, Hashem attaches Himself to us. If we exhibit a grief stricken countenance, Hashem sends misfortune to maintain our woeful veneer. When a person smiles at Hashem, Hashem reciprocates by giving him more reasons to smile. If a person praises Hashem as the healer of all flesh, Hashem opens the gates of healing for him.

The Baal HaTanya once overheard his grandson, the Tzemach Tzedek, davening with a sad tune. After he finished praying, he told him in the name of his great teacher, the Maggid of Mezrich, that the response from above reflects our input below. One must avoid sad niggunim, particularly during prayer, for they evoke distressing rejoinders.

The Ari writes that it is forbidden to pray when depressed.

Despair blocks the spiritual light that is aroused by one's prayer. Prayers tinged with despair will not accomplish much.

When a poor man begs the king for money, he is only given a small sum, no matter how much he cries. But when a prince praises the king while presenting his petition, he will receive generous gifts as befits his status. (Tzavaas HaRivash)

Worry and sadness about matters of this world enfeeble our appeal to Hashem. If we make an effort to substitute joy for our fears – approaching Hashem with exuberance, like the prince – Hashem will surely help us.[43]

Because joy in prayer is so important, we are advised to pray in a place with windows.[44] Darkness causes depression and anxiety, while light results in contentment and gladness.

If one's heart is filled with a rush of joy and love for Hashem during one's prayers, it is a sign that Hashem has chosen to fulfill his wishes, as it says, "And find delight in Hashem and He will grant you the desires of your heart." *(Tehillim 37,4)*

When people came to R' Yehoshua Leib, the Brisker Rav, asking him to pray for a sick person, he sometimes offered a brief prayer on the spot and at other times went on to give advice. Numerous stories indicate that he always knew whether the ill person would recover or not. (Amud HaEsh)

R' Eliyahu Lapian would pray regularly on behalf of others. His students noticed that he would sometimes sort through the notes with individual names and place selected ones into the back of the siddur. The students later confirmed that the names in the back no longer required prayers.

One Thursday a telegram was received from America asking that R' Eliyahu daven on behalf of R' Nosson Wachtfogel, who had been diagnosed with a serious illness and would soon be undergoing surgery.

On Shabbos morning R' Eliyahu commented, "Wachtfogel is healthy." When asked how he knew, he refused to answer. Later it was discovered that R' Nosson had immediately recovered. (Lev Eliyahu)

When a surge of ecstasy occurs when one is not praying, one should cherish the precious moment. This wonderful flash of passionate Divine love is similar to the revelations of the prophets of old.

In an expansive mood after a daily study session with his grandson, R' Yosef Chaim Sonnenfeld began reminiscing about his rebbe, the Ksav Sofer. Transported back to his early years, he began singing the prayer Elokai Neshama to the Hungarian tune his rebbe had used. When he came to the phrase "Kol zman shehaneshama bekirbi modeh ani lefanecha – So long as my soul is within me I give thanks before You," he entered such a state of ecstasy that it seemed as if his body was in danger of losing its grip on his soul. (HaIsh al HaChomah)

The Piasetzna Rebbe taught the importance of taking

advantage of our emotions. When we experience moments of animation, sadness, joy or anxiety, we should find the opportunity to pray as soon as possible. He recommends reciting Tehillim that have some bearing on your situation. He writes, "If you are worried about your competitors, say the verse, 'How great are my troubles, O G–d, everyone rises against me.' (Tehillim 3,2) If you are feeling upset with no specific cause, you could recite, 'I am swept up in a wave of despair,' (Tehillim 6,1) or 'I will raise up my eyes to the mountains from where will flow my salvation.' (Tehillim 121,1)"

Enthusiastic Prayer

If our prayers are to be worthy of the name, they must be vibrant and enthusiastic – not stilted and indifferent. During the course of the day we should think about how Hashem's glory fills the whole universe, and how we ourselves exist within Him and His holiness. The more often we reflect on these matters of faith, the easier it will be to stimulate our souls to speak to Hashem.[46]

A person should consider that there is so much to be accomplished during the course of a lifetime, and the ultimate judgment is searing. Only Hashem can help us. Now is the time to cry out for assistance. This should help us vault the hurdle of indifference, and give vibrancy to our prayers.[47]

Even though our enthusiasm may not initially be wholehearted, if we persist in our efforts then our heart will ignite with Hashem's exaltation, and we will be worthy of praying with real fervor.[48] Even when a person feels that he cannot draw close to Hashem, in an instant the light that shines from above can kindle his soul.[49] We start with asking Hashem for what we need. While we pray, our soul will be awakened and will begin to long for unity with the King of kings. Our activated soul enables us to pray with passion, not only when we are praying for personal needs but also when we are focused on G–dly matters.[50]

Every year on the day before Rosh Chodesh Shevat R' Yaakov Mutzapi would refrain from speaking (taanis dibur). He would initiate the prayers that day with the Vidui of Yom Kippur with tearful emotion. He would say the book of Tehillim three times with passionate enthusiasm, followed by Mincha. R' Yaakov raised his voice and personally pleaded with Hashem to pardon the Jewish people to the accompaniment of plentiful sobbing. After Maariv he would individually bless each of the participants. Everyone present returned home with great joy. (Ari Alah MiBavel)

Avoiding Fixed Prayer

"Fixed prayer" refers to prayer which is viewed as a burden.[51] Each prayer should be perceived as a distinct opportunity for spiritual growth. Each day should bring a new attempt at elevating another emotional component of our makeup. Just as one day differs qualitatively from the next, so should our prayers reflect daily growth and improve dramatically from day to day. Man should seek to apply his life experience to a new understanding of his prayer.

We should focus on one concept one day and another the next day. Greatness, Divine Providence, thankfulness, the glories of Hashem's beautiful world – all are possible themes. In the course of our reading, we should search for different thoughts to append to the words of prayer. Because our understanding of the world is in constant flux, we will thereby bring a fresh new perspective to what we say each day.[52]

Tefilah is referred to with ten different words in the Hebrew language, reflecting the divergent characteristics of prayer and corresponding to man's diversified experiences, with the broad spectrum of his heart's response.[53] In every given situation it is possible to employ all the different modes of prayers. When Moshe *Rabbeinu* davened 515 times, he employed 515 types of prayer.[54] Each prayer was different from the next. Although Moshe prayed to Hashem for forty days and nights, his prayers remained as fervent at the end of the period as at the beginning.[55] Moshe Rabbeinu's unchanging ardor is what made his *tefilah* so beloved by Hashem.[56]

When R' Shmuel Kowalksky was looking for a son-in-law, he would check out the prospective chassan's Shabbos davening. He felt that praying with intensity in the main body of the Shabbos tefillos was not enough. He observed whether the young man said the Shir Kavod after Musaf with enthusiasm and the Anim Zemiros with warmth, for these elevated prayers are usually hastily executed.

A young man approached Rabbi Kowalsky, asking to

become a member of the Sochatchov Kollel. When the man arrived, Rabbi Kowalsky was learning and could not be interrupted. Before they could speak it was time to daven Maariv. After their prayers, Rabbi Kowalsky told the young man that he was accepted. Those present were astonished. Consideration as a Kollel member normally followed a forbidding oral entry exam, which tested the breadth of the applicant's knowledge. Rabbi Kowalsky explained that the young man had passed another sort of entry exam with flying colors. Rabbi Kowalsky had observed him during evening prayers, and concluded that he was the right candidate for the position. (Ana Avda)

Entreaty for Mercy

The *Mishnah* recommends that our prayers be an entreaty for mercy and a supplication before the Omnipresent.[57] Man should pray in a beseeching manner, like a pauper pleading at the door. It is only due to G–d's loving kindness that He gives us the opportunity to approach Him in prayer.[58] This is the intent of the words of the *Nishmas* prayer, "Until now Your mercy has helped us, and Your kindness has not forsaken us. Do not abandon us, Hashem, our G–d, forever."

R' Aryeh Tzvi Frumer, the Gaon from Koziglov, would begin his preparations for his morning prayers the night before. He would wake up and say Tikun Chatzos with much weeping and then study until the light of day. During that *period he did not speak but would motion with his hands if he needed something.*

His preparation for Shabbos prayers began at Mincha, which he would daven with tears streaming down his face, but without moving. At Kabolas Shabbos he was like a flaming torch. When his students wished him "gut Shabbos" after davening, his lips responded while his thoughts remained in elevated spheres.

The pinnacle of his service was the Nishmas prayer on Shabbos morning. It took him half an hour or longer. He caressed each individual word. His yearning for Hashem's closeness was apparent to all. Whoever witnessed his Nishmas never forgot it. (Eleh Eskera, volume I)

Hashem's compassion is boundless and can never be depleted by our sins. This concept is cited by the *Zohar (1,90)* on the verse, "And he trusted in Hashem and he reckoned it to him as righteousness." *(Bereishis 15,6)*[59] Avraham was not afraid that his sins would negate Hashem's promises, because he knew he could rely on His compassion.[60]

If a person is being threatened and appeals to Hashem to save him, he must first acknowledge that it is his evil deeds that prevent the realization of his goals. The Torah warns us what to avoid and advises us which path to pursue. Three times a day we repeat Hashem's warning not to stray.[61] When the punishment ultimately materializes, how can we turn to Hashem to save us from the difficulties which we brought upon ourselves? Clearly it can only be a supplication based on Hashem's unlimited compassion. We appeal for an act of grace, pleading for a favor as a slave before his master.

The author of the *Shulchan Aruch* notes that it is important to realize that we do not deserve to have Hashem fulfill our requests.[62] We should therefore ask that Hashem respond to our entreaties with mercy and not justice,[63] solely as an act of grace.[64]

Why do we avoid prayers that are based on merit, choosing to make our prayers an appeal for mercy? Certainly we have good deeds and charitable acts! Yet the supply of merit for good deeds is limited by the amount of good deeds we perform. Often our good deeds are tainted and the reward minimized. G–d's grace, on the others hand, is bound to His compassion, which is pure and unlimited.[65]

Our prayers must plead with Hashem to grant us that which we need as a gift, and not rely on favors based on our good deeds. Chizkiyahu pleaded for help in his merit, yet Hashem granted it in the merit of Dovid. Moshe, in contrast, asked for a gift, and Hashem granted his request.[66]

Before requesting anything during the course of the day, one should first praise Hashem, as our sages advised, "A person should prepare praises of Hashem and then pray." *(Berachos 32)* After Hashem fulfills his request, he should praise Hashem for each gift.[67] Beginning our prayers with praises of Hashem makes it clear that Hashem does not owe anything to us; whatever we receive is a gift.[68] We should therefore rejoice with anything that comes our way.[69]

Rabbi Shlomo Zalmen Auerbach would instruct educators to explain to their students that not all prayers are answered. We ask our Heavenly Father for compassion, and rely on Hashem to give the response that is best for us. "Who amongst Your creations… can say to You, 'What are You doing and what are You accomplishing?' Our Father in Heaven, living and enduring One, do kindness with us."[70] It is not our responsibility to give Hashem specific instructions; rather, we should beseech that His compassion should be visible to us.[71]

The Rambam sees tefillah as an opportunity to contemplate the nature and grandeur of Hashem. This contemplation leads to the establishment of a bond with the Divine. By pondering Hashem's works, man recognizes His infinite wisdom and comes to love Him. It also serves to make man cognizant of his puny intelligence and flawed nature, and puts him in a proper frame of mind to plead for G-d's mercy. (Rambam, Yesodei HaTorah 2,2)

[1] Orach Chaim 93:2

[2] Berachos 30

[3] Binah LeIttim Derush 16

[4] Tehilim 44,23; R' Nachman's wisdom # 12

[5] Last Will and Testament of the Baal Shem Tov

[6] Rabenu Bachya Bamidbar 16,22

[7] Lev Dovid

[8] Bais Tefillah

[9] Rambam beginning of the laws of Tefillah; Kesav VeKabalah Shemos 9,29

[10] Sotah 5a

[11] Chovos HaLevavos, Shaar Cheshbon HaNefesh 9, with commentary Lev Tov

[12] Alei Shor, Part I

[13] Mishlei 21,27

[14] Gra

[15] Introduction to Tefillas Chana, Rabbi Reuven Melamed, based on Yevamos 64

[16] Yalkut Sippurim

[17] Shearim BeTefillah, Nipul

[18] Berachos 34

[19] Shearim BeTefillah, Nipul

[20] Yaaros Devash Derush One

[21] Bais Elokim, Shaar HaTefilla 8

[22] Rashi on Divrei Hayamim II 7,14

[23] Alshich HaKadosh

[24] Tiferes Shlomo, Vayigash

[25] Degel Machane Efraim

[26] Adapted from Imrei Pinchas

[27] Shevet Sofer, chapter 16,31

[28] Emunah, pages 182-183

[29] Temurah 16; Divrei HaYamim I 4,10

[30] Rashi on Tehillim 143,9

31 Rosh Hashanah, chapter 3

32 Berachos 31

33 Sefer HaChassidim

34 Divrei HaYamim I 29, 17-18; Mesilas Yesharim 19

35 Charedim

36 Tefillas Chana

37 Introduction to Tefillas Chana

38 Lev Shalom, Parshas VaYeshev

39 Mesilas Yesharim 19

40 Nefesh HaChaim 2,13

41 Bais Tefillah

42 Reishis Chochmah, Ahava 10,17

43 Bais Tefillah

44 Berachos 31

45 Birkas Aharon

46 Chovos HaTalmidim, chapter 9

47 Shearim BeTefillah, Bitzur

48 Sichos Haran 66,74

49 Likutim Yekarim 3d

50 Chovos HaTalmidim, chapter 9

51 Berachos 29a

52 Toldos Yaakov Yosef, Ekev 3; Bais Tefillah

53 Shearim BeTefillah, Rabbi Pinkus

54 Aderes Eliyahu

55 Or Chodosh

56 R' Ephraim Zaitchek

57 Avos 2,18

58 Shulchan Aruch, Orach Chaim 98

59 Zohar, Terumah 143

60 Gra

[61] Shema

[62] Orach Chaim 98; Ari HaKadosh as recorded by R' Chaim Vital

[63] Rabenu Bachya

[64] Kli Yakar

[65] Adapted from Shearim BeTefillah, Tachanunim

[66] Sefer HaYashar IV, chapter 21

[67] Kuntres HaTzavah

[68] Olelos Ephraim

[69] Mishnas Rebbe Aharon

[70] Shacharis prayer

[71] Halichos Shlomo

Prayer in Action

Practical Techniques

Developing the proper attitude towards prayer is a first important step. Yet how does one translate these feelings into practice? Prayer involves both inward concentration and the outward manifestation of these thoughts. The way one stands, the length of one's prayer, the tears one sheds during *tefilah* – all are indications of the depth of feeling a person has achieved in his communication with Hashem.

Praying with Tears

Blessed is the person who always prays with tears, for his prayers are heard. The letters of the *Amidah* prayer can be rearranged to spell *dimah*, tears. Our *Shemoneh Esrei* prayer is guaranteed to be effective when we pray with tears.[1] Often a person is not worthy of having his prayers accepted, but because he consistently cries and pleads with Hashem to help him, he is saved.[2]

A man who prays with heartfelt devotion possesses the key that opens the gates of Heaven. Tears are like an axe that breaks through all gates.[3] There is no gate that stays closed to tears.[4] Hashem gathers each and every tear, adds them up, and stores them for emergencies.[5] The Gates of Tears were never sealed, for tears are in the place of the "water libations" that were offered in the holy Temple on the altar.[6] The angels in charge of the gates of tears will leave their posts to escort tearful prayers upwards.[7]

The Ropshitzer Rebbe questions the need for a gate if the gate of tears is always open. He answers his own question by explaining that it is closed against tears of an unworthy nature. Why shed tears that fall to the ground when one can shed tears that rise to heaven?

> When news of the brutal murder of the Jews of Europe reached Eretz Yisrael, R' Sulamon Mutzapi and others headed to Kever Rochel. The first half of the night they studied. The second half was devoted to prayers and entreaties on behalf of the Jews of Europe. Their wailing echoed through the town.

> When a small number of refugees began arriving in Eretz Yisrael, "fragments saved from the fire," R' Sulamon once again assembled a large group to pray on behalf of their suffering brethren. When he arrived at Kever Rochel with his entourage, the Arabs called out, "The criers have arrived."

> In the years 1949-1950 the Jews of Baghdad were persecuted because many Jews had applied for exit visas so that they might settle in Israel. Rabbi Mutzapi organized a day of prayer at the Kosel. He donned sackcloth, put ash on his

head and sat on the ground, crying and wailing together with many men, women and children who had joined him. They prayed on behalf of these hapless Jews through the night. Two days later they found out that the Jews of Iraq had been given permission to emigrate. As a result more then one hundred thousand Jews moved to Eretz Yisrael. (Olamo shel Tzadik)

For years Reb Raphael of Brisk fought against the policy of forced autopsies in Eretz Yisrael. With a loyal crew of assistants he organized demonstrations, furtively buried the dead, and fought to retrieve body parts, while at the same time trying to alter government policy on this sensitive issue. He told his daughter about the most powerful weapon in his arsenal. "I don't need a million people. I need a few old ladies in Yerushalayim who pray tearfully." (The Life and Times of Reb Raphael Soloveitchik, page 220)

Why are tears so effective? Tears are the expression of our innermost soul, an outgrowth of our essence. Heartfelt prayer is a weak force in comparison to the surge of emotion that produces tears. Because tears originate at such an exclusive source, it readily opens the gates of Heaven.[8]

An abundance of tears aids concentration and results in a stronger attachment to Hashem.[9] If a person finds it difficult to cry, he should pray in a hushed spasmodic voice, as if he were crying.[10]

As a child, R' Baruch Ber Levovitz was disciplined by his father and began to cry. Still crying, he reached for his Siddur and turned to the Mincha prayers. His father asked why he wanted to daven Mincha now. The youngster replied that if he was crying anyway, then he wished to dedicate his tears to prayer. (Shearim BeTefillah, Neaka)

Prayer requires tears of submission, which are only a rung away from tears of joy.[11] These two emotions should alternate. We are joyous because we are privileged to stand before Hashem and bring pleasure to His Majesty. Yet we are regretful when we consider how much we have sinned and how little we have accomplished.[12] The acronym of the verse, "In your name they will rejoice all the day" *(Tehillim 89)* spell *bechiya*, tears. We feel sad at being distant from Hashem, yet happy to be able to praise and serve Him.[13]

When the Tzemach Tzaddik of Vizhnitz davened Tachanun, a puddle of tears and sweat would form where he stood. He clearly relished his prayers. One Shavuos after davening he turned to his chassidim and said, "Until now we have fulfilled the 'half unto ourselves;' now let us fulfill the 'half unto Hashem.'" Having luxuriated in his prayers, he would now turn his attention to his obligation to Hashem by eating the holiday meal for the sake of Heaven. (Tzemach Tzaddik)

Leah shed many tears in the hope that she would wed the righteous Yaakov and not the wicked Esav. Despite the fact that she was destined for Esav, her tears enabled her to wed Yaakov. This teaches us that copious tears can rend a bad decree asunder.[14] Chana, too, prayed to Hashem, "and cried and cried." *(Shmuel 1,10)*[15] Her tear-drenched entreaties had an effect; as the verse specifies later, her prayer was accepted.[16]

Aware of the power of tears, *Dovid Hamelech* said, "Hear my prayer, G-d, hearken to my call, be not deaf to my tears." *(Tehillim 39,13)* Similarly, we find in reference to King Chizkiyahu's prayers, "And Chizkiyahu cried, and G—d said to him, 'I have heard your prayer, I have seen your tears.'" *(Melachim II 20)*

When Rochel prayed for her descendants, she cried on their behalf, mevakah al baneha. Hashem responded to her tears and said, "'Stop your voice from crying and your eyes from tears for your efforts will be rewarded,' swore Hashem, 'and they will return from exile. …Your sons will return to their boundaries.'" *(Eichah Rabba)*[17]

People would approach the Chozeh after Yom Kippur to ask what had been decreed for the year ahead. Many were given the information they sought. One year the Chozeh told the Rebbe Reb Bunim that he would lose all his money in the coming year. And so it was. His wife and several children fell sick, and he had to use his entire fortune of nearly fifteen thousand rubles on doctors and medicines.

When they had all recovered, he traveled to Warsaw in the hope that Hashem would send him some means of supporting his family. He checked into a hotel and waited. The weeks passed, the bills started to accumulate and he had not a penny in his pocket. He worried about the chilul Hashem that would result when it was discovered that he had no funds to pay for his accommodations. He was so distressed that he began to cry.

He cried and cried until someone knocked on the door. It was a messenger from the famous philanthropist Tamarel. She wanted to employ him for six rubles a week. When the Rebbe Reb Bunim heard the offer, it seemed to him that Hashem was once again opening the doors of sustenance. He told the messenger that he was not interested in working for her boss; he wanted to become her partner. Tamarel was angered by his response and did not communicate with him further.

The Rebbe Reb Bunim was not perturbed in the slightest. He sat down to learn as always. A week later Tamarel agreed to his condition and asked him to come to her office to discuss the details. She paid all his debts and gave him his first assignment.

When he saw the Chozeh of Lublin again, the Chozeh commented, "What I told you was accurate, but tears were not in the picture." The Rebbe Reb Bunim's tears had annulled the decree.

Length of Prayer

The length of a prayer is not important, as Hashem told Moshe, "There is a time to pray at length, and a time to be brief." *(Mechilta Shemos 14:15)* Both a long and short prayer may be of the same value and have the same effect. When Moshe *davened* for all of *bnei Yisrael* he *davened* at length. There was not a single corner in heaven in which Moshe R*abbeinu* did not pray.[18] But when he *davened* for his sister, he was very brief.[19]

Our Rabbis tell of a certain disciple who spun out his prayer while davening in the presence of Rabbi Eliezer. The other disciples said to their master, "How long winded the fellow is." He replied to them, "Is he drawing it out any more than our master Moshe, of whom it is written, 'So I fell down before the Lord forty days and forty nights' (Devarim 9,25)?" Another time a certain disciple was very brief. His disciples said, "How concise this fellow is," to which Rabbi Eliezer replied, "Is he any more concise than our master Moshe, who briefly requested, 'Heal her now, O G–d I beseech You.' (Bamidbar 12)?" (Berachos 34a)

There are two approaches to prayer: praying slowly as if one were counting money, or speedy prayer with no delay between words.

A proponent of the swift approach defends this theory by comparing it to an owner of an orchard, who decided to set up a fence around his property to prevent animals from plundering his fruit. He will achieve his goal only if the stakes are placed close together. If he leaves a space between the stakes, his fence will be useless. A person who pauses between words during prayer gives stray thoughts the opportunity to vex him.

His friend claimed that his analogy worked only when the pests were outside the orchard. If the animals were already inside, he could never get rid of them if the posts were close together. When a person is in the midst of prayer, he must slow down and carefully pluck stray thoughts from his mind.[20]

The Rebbe of Rizhin used to daven at great length, while the Belzer Rebbe davened quickly. Both were equally devoted to their prayers. The Rabbi of Rizhin loved the prayers so fervently that he hardly could let them go, and therefore clung to every word. The Rabbi of Belz, on the other hand, had such a passion for prayer that he impatiently swallowed the words, longing to grasp them as quickly as possible. His love of G–d was burning in his heart so strongly that the words left his mouth of their own accord. (Judaism Thoughts and Legends)

Rabbi Akiva would daven briefly when davening with others, but when he davened alone he would start on one side of the shul and end up at the other side, because of his long, involved prayer filled with genuflection and prostration. (Berachos 31)

Some experts in the art of prayer may choose to *daven* briefly. "When the love of Hashem burns strongly in one's heart, the words leave one's mouth of their own accord while you pray silently. At these times one finds oneself *davening* quickly." *(Tzavaas HaRivash)*

Praying quickly is not an indication that a person takes prayer lightly. Rav Shraga Feivel Mendlowitz compared prayer to mountain climbing. A mountain climber exerts tremendous effort to reach the summit. Once there, however, he strolls around with ease. When a person invests a great deal of effort to prepare for an encounter with the Almighty, his prayer will spring unimpeded from his heart and flow smoothly from his lips. He will be focused on the task at hand and will not stumble and hesitate over the words. Far from being an indication that one considers prayer trivial, alacrity may actually show how devoted he is.[21]

Prayer has been compared to a sword and a bow.[22] A proficient archer requires only one arrow to reach his target; a practiced swordsman knows exactly where to land a deadly blow.[23] When a man knows the address, he aims one sharp arrow, straight and true, at the target.[24]

R' Chaim `Ozer Grodzinsky would daven swiftly. Sometimes he would have to wait for the chazan to finish the Amidah prayer. While he prayed red stains would appear on his forehead. Knowledgeable doctors explained that they resulted from R' Chaim Ozer straining to contain the hundreds of thoughts that vied for his attention so he could focus on his prayers. (Amud HaTefillah)

The Lubliner Rebbe asked his disciple, the Yehudi HaKadosh, why he gobbled his prayer. He answered, "The words are so dear to me and I desire to swallow them as quickly as possible." The Lubliner Rav replied "Are not the words of tefillah dear to me, too? But they are like a burning flame and hard to swallow." (Sipurei Chassidim)

When the Chasam Sofer's students commented on his lengthy prayers, he told them that he never viewed his prayers as being long. His own Rebbe, R' Noson Adler, would still be davening Arvis of Kabolas Shabbos when his students rejoined him after eating their seudah. He said, "We didn't hurry with our davening, but we had enough time to daven and eat and return to find him still engrossed in his prayers." (Heard by R' Shimon Sofer from his father the Ksav Sofer, see Introduction to Siddur Chasam Sofer)

In the days when there were no direct flights from Switzerland to Eretz Yisroel, the Brisker Rav and his son Raphael had to change planes in Rome. On the flight there was a Jew who had yahrzeit. Since there were ten Jews present, they put together a minyan for Mincha. As the group started Shemoneh Esrei, they announced that the plane for Tel Aviv was boarding immediately. Missing a plane in Rome in those days was no small matter. It meant staying in Rome overnight, if not longer. Everyone hurried his Shemoneh Esrei, the chazan said his part very quickly, and everyone ran to the airplane. The Brisker Rav continued praying Shemoneh Esrei as calmly as ever, saying every word slowly and clearly, as usual. Reb Raphael was getting nervous because everyone had boarded the plane and he heard the engines switch on.

He began considering their options. Where would they stay overnight in Rome? Would there be seats available on the next day's flight? Reb Raphael watched the steward stretching out his hand to close the cabin door, and he turned to his father who was still davening slowly and calmly. Reb Raphael then noticed a priest who motioned to the steward to wait for the Brisker Rav. They all sat and waited for the Brisker Rav to finish Shemoneh Esrei. When he finished, Reb Raphael told him that everyone had boarded and they were waiting for him. The Brisker Rov walked to the plane and took his seat; the door was closed and the plane immediately took off. (*The Life and Times of Reb Raphael Soloveitchik*, page 154)

R' Yechiel Mayer of Ostrovza's prayers could melt a heart of stone. When times were difficult for the Jews, he would spend three hours on each prayer. During World War I, he shed copious tears on behalf of the Jewish people. When approached by a chassid with the name of another person enduring terrible suffering, the Rebbe replied, "Please don't mention his name. The Jewish people are drowning in a sea of suffering, I don't have the emotional stamina to pray on behalf of one suffering individual." (*Marbitzei Torah MeOlam HaChassidus*)

A wise man was once asked how long one should pray *Shemoneh Esrei.* He replied, "Until one finishes." Unfortunately, many people rush through their prayers. Often they arrive at *shul* late and must speed to catch up. Others who arrive on time may be restricted by the *chazan* who *davens* hurriedly. As soon as the prayers are officially over they rush off.

A person would be very insulted if he asked a friend for a few minutes to discuss something and the friend said, "I have no time for you." Yet we do not hesitate to indicate the same attitude in our communications with Hashem. We throw in a few words, "I need life, sustenance, health," and then we hurriedly wind up, take off our tefillin and flee. The way to rectify this situation is to arrive early.

Prayers are not a chore to get over with. You should concentrate on every word that comes out of your mouth. If you have to plead and request something from a human king, would he grant your wish if you presented it in haste? In all likelihood the king would have you thrown out for your disregard of proper decorum. Showing reverence for the King of kings requires that we show proper respect by stating our case with care.

When Rabbi Eliezer Yitzchak of Volozhin saw a student who davened quickly, he called him in to tell him how important it is to pray with concentration.

"Rebbe, let me explain myself," said the student. "Imagine a man traveling in a cart. If the cart goes too slowly, all types of creatures jump onto it. If the cart travels very fast, however, nothing can jump on the court. When I pray slowly all types of foreign thoughts enter my head, whereas when I daven quickly, I don't have that problem."

"I'm afraid, however," said Rabbi Eliezer Yitzchak, "that when you daven as fast as you do, you yourself may be one of the creatures that doesn't manage to jump onto the cart." (A Touch of Wisdom, A Touch of Wit, Prayer)

To Learn or to Pray?

The *Or Zaruah* maintained that a person should lengthen his prayer even at the expense of Torah study. One who does not *daven* because he is teaching Torah to others is considered not to have studied at all.[25] The Torah studied by a person who does not take his *davening* seriously is no more significant than Torah studied by a gentile; it is simply an intellectual exercise.[26]

R' Yehuda HaChassid told of a great rabbi and teacher who soundly rebuked his fellow congregants for spending too much time *davening* at the expense of their studies. He was punished severely for this indiscretion.[27]

The Chasam Sofer was asked why he took so much time praying when he could be spending that time studying Torah. He replied that whoever takes his time davening has his days lengthened, and he will therefore have time to study more. (A Touch of Wisdom, A Touch of Wit, Prayer)

A very talented young man who had been very studious suddenly decided to leave the Lakewood Kollel. To everyone's surprise, he started a business. The Mashgiach, R' Noson Wachtfogel, was quick to point out that the young man didn't devote enough time to his prayers, and therefore his dedication to his studies had been impaired. (Memoirs of R' Noson Wachtfogel)

Praying Aloud

Prayer is an exercise in intimacy, a private conversation between a son and his father, man and his Maker; loudness and shouting are uncalled for. One who concentrates all his thoughts and senses on this private conversation with the Almighty attains true intimacy with the Divine, as if he were alone with Hashem his Father, "Like a sparrow that is alone on the house top." *(Tehillim 102,8)* This cogent prayer flows in a secret communion between one who is alone with himself and G–d.

A rabbi who was visiting the Bais HaLevi shouted his prayers at the top of his lungs. When the visitor was walking his host home, the Bais HaLevi yelled into his ear, "There's something important I want to tell you."

The man replied, "Rebbe, I am right here beside you. There is no need to shout."

The Bais Halevi replied, "The verse tells us that Hashem, too, is close to those that call him. Why do you scream so loudly when you pray?" (Yalkut Avodah Be'Tefilah)

On the other hand, praying loud enough for our ears to hear helps us concentrate better.[28] Raising our voice can improve our kavanah. We are told that calling out to Hashem works both before a decree and after.[29]

One Yom Tov the Baal Shem Tov led the prayers. He prayed with fiery devotion, shouting the words with all his might. The Maggid of Mezrich, who was sickly, was rattled by the cries and decided to continue his prayers in a small room attached to the shul.

Before Musaf, the Baal Shem Tov came into the room where the Maggid was praying to get his kittel. The Maggid observed that the Divine Presence hovered over the Besht, who seemed to be in another world. The Maggid reached out to help his Rebbe don his kittel. As soon as he touched the Besht, the Maggid began to tremble. He tried to steady himself on the table, which also began to tremble. He had to pray to Hashem to withdraw the Holy spirit from him, for he did not possess the strength to deal with it. (Shivchei HaBesht)

The Chazon Ish would go to the Bais Midrash very early, before anyone else arrived. Because he davened slowly, he would start his prayer alone. He prayed with fiery enthusiasm, joyfully enunciating each letter, his voice echoing through the shul. As soon as the first person arrived, he would lower his voice and continue his prayer in a more restrained fashion. (Pe'er HaDor)

Movement in Prayer

There is no definitive recommendation in regard to movement in prayer. According to the *Menoras HaMaor*, shaking while praying is the custom of the pious. The *Chavos Yair* recommends that a person shake his hands and body to and fro with great strength as he prays.[30]

Rabbi Menachem de Lunzano was of the opinion that shaking while praying disturbs a person's concentration. Standing without movement during prayer enables one to concentrate better. "Does anyone make a request of a human king with his body swaying like trees of the forest in the wind?" he asks.

> *R' Moshe Feinstein would stand motionless during Shemoneh Esrei, except when bowing. He explained that when the Communists interrogated him in Luban he had been forced to stand at attention, as a guard stood watch. Never had he felt so subservient. From then on he decided that he would demonstrate his subservience to the true Ruler by standing this way during Shemoneh Esrei. (Reb Moshe)*

Generally the *Baal Shem Tov* recommended movement in prayer. "When a person is drowning and thrashes about to save himself, people certainly will not make fun of his motions. Similarly, when a person makes motions during prayer, one should not laugh at him. He is saving himself from drowning in the waters of insolence."[31]

Elsewhere the *Baal Shem Tov* talks of praying with love and awe and with great intensity that is not visible on the body. A person who closely binds himself to Hashem with his entire soul does not need to move. An observer might think he is merely reciting the words without any feeling, but in reality he is drawing nearer and nearer to Hashem. Such prayer, which is all inside, is inaccessible to evil forces that try to prevent one from praying with devotion.[32]

The *Mishnah Berurah (48,5)* cites both sides of the argument and concludes that everyone should do according to his own nature. If he can concentrate better while swaying, he should sway, and if not he should stand still.

When R' Avraham Matisyahu of Shtefinesht would daven he was totally oblivious to his surroundings. Once R' Betzalel Zeev Shafran entered his private room while the Rebbe was praying. To his horror he saw that the kerosene lamp had filled the entire room with smoke, so the Rebbe's face was all black. The Rebbe, totally oblivious to what was happening, was still standing and praying intensely.

The Rivnitzer Rebbe testified that even in his last years the Rebbe of Shtefinesht would daven for hours, standing without moving a limb. Only one sigh would escape his lips. In the last year of his life he sighed twice. (Halichos Tefilah)

Proper Posture

When a person *davens* he should stand at attention like a soldier, anxious to obey the command of his leader. He should not heed his aches and pains, nor think about his problems.

Rabbi Yitzchak Silberstein was once at Tel HaShomer hospital when suddenly two heavily armed men entered the waiting room with their guns raised. Everyone was asked to leave the room. Not daring to argue with a raised weapon, all present hurriedly left the room.

The armed men were Brink's security company representatives who had come to empty the bank machine in the lobby. As they were emptying it, a man approached one of the Brink employees, clapped him on the back, and called out, "Aharon! How are you doing? So good to see you."

The man motioned to his friend to leave and then continued with his task. He would not be distracted. Only after the job was done and the money safely deposited in the armored truck did he seek out his friend and apologize. The two then caught up on the latest news.

Rabbi Silberstein was deeply impressed by what he had witnessed. If only our devotion to our prayers was comparable to the commitment of Brink's employees! If only we would recognize the seriousness of our responsibility to Hashem and act accordingly! (Tuvcha Yabiu)

When praying, one should fold his hands on his chest, the right over the left. This is the posture of a servant before his master.[33] Hands on the hips or on the waist symbolize pride and are unacceptable.[34]

Lowering one's eyes is an aid to achieving the proper frame of mind. This narrows one's frame of reference so that everything extraneous is blocked out. This is particularly important if one is readily distracted by the activities of others.[35]

Some recommend praying with closed eyes in order to concentrate better.[36] Others maintain that one must pray every word from a *siddur*.[37]

The Alter of Kelm was very weak. He kept small cookies nearby to nibble on so he would not pass out during Shemoneh Esrei. Because he had no strength, he sought the smallest Esrog available. Despite his infirmity, he davened at length from a siddur.

One day, in the middle of Shacharis, he walked to the back of the shul, opened a siddur, glanced inside and then returned to his place. One word was missing in his siddur; he had read the word from a different one to maintain his commitment to always pray from a siddur. (Moreshes Avos)

From a young age Rabbi Halberstam, the Klausenberger Rebbe, prayed with such fervor that he awed all who observed his devotions. It was difficult to stand near him as he prayed Shemoneh Esrei without being moved to tears. At the age of nine he undertook to say Tikun Chatzos at midnight every day. He would steal into the shul, open the Aron Kodesh and pour out his heart to Hashem.

One night, his cries reached a neighbor's ears. The man concluded that the wailing was not human. Despite his fear, he was determined to investigate. He was astonished to discover the young son of the Rav standing near the Aron, crying profusely with his arms outstretched. To hear the young child confess his sins and beg for forgiveness and heavenly assistance with his studies moved the man to his core. "If this young child cries over his 'sins', what should I say?" he thought.

The midnight episode gave him no respite. He could not get the scene out of his mind. Ultimately, he became a baal teshuvah. When the Rebbe's father heard the story, he asked that it be kept from his son for fear that he would become conceited.

As a young man the Rebbe would jump about and dance with great emotion as he prayed. His movements caused the floorboards to crack and separate. He wanted to hire someone to repair the floor, but was stopped by the members of the Kleinverdein shul. They said, "Leave the cracks so we can show our children how Reb Zalmen Leibele (as his father fondly called him) prayed."

On a visit to Munkatch, the Rebbe davened Shacharis as was his habit. The Munkatcher Rebbe, the Munchas Eluzar, asked how far he had reached. When he was told VaYivorech Dovid, he asked, "Is he still saying 'VaYevorech' or has he already begun to say 'Dovid?'" (Lapid Esh)

[1] Yaaros Devash

[2] Sefer HaChassidim Chapter 130

[3] Beer Moshe Ekev

[4] Zohar

[5] Shabbos 105,2

[6] Bereishis Rabah, Shaar HaAvodah of Rabenu Yona

[7] Beer Moshe Parshas Ekev

[8] Or Chodosh Parshas VaEschanan

[9] Ralbag Shmuel 1,7

[10] Shaloh HaKadosh Maseches Tamid

[11] Zohar, Part III 75,1

[12] Peleh Yoetz

[13] Likutei Maharan 175

[14] Zohar, Parshas VaYechi, page 223

[15] Rabbeinu Bachya, Kad HaKemach

[16] Ralbag Shmuel I 7,15

[17] Pninei R' Yechezkel

[18] Midrash Tehillim 90,6

[19] Bamidbar 12:13; Zohar 2,244b

[20] HaMayan HaNitzchi, page 93

[21] HaMashgiach MiKaminetz

[22] Mechilta Bereishis 48,22; Bava Kama 123

[23] Sanhedrin 49, discussing Shmuel 2,2

[24] Shearim BeTefillah, Kriah

[25] Rokeach cited by Mishnah Berurah 106

[26] from a discourse by R' Menachem Shach

[27] Or Zaruah, Hilchos Shabbos 1

[28] Tur, Orach Chaim 98

[29] Rosh Hashana 18, see Ran

[30] Mekor Chaim 95,2

[31] Likutim Yekarim 66

[32] Tzavaas HaRivash

[33] Orach Chaim 95,63

[34] Beer Moshe Parshas Ekev

[35] Reishis Chochmah, Shaar HaKedusha, chapter 8

[36] Sefer HaYashar, Shaar 13

[37] Vilna Gaon, Chofetz Chaim, Rav Moshe Feinstein

Directing our Prayers

Davening with Kavanah

The numerical equivalent of *tefillah*, prayer, is *be'kavanah*, which means "with *kavanah*."[1] The word kavanah is usually translated as "concentration," "intention" or "devotion." It is characterized by love or awe of Hashem.

The origin of the word *kavanah* comes from the Hebrew root *kave*, which means to aim. *Kavanah* denotes aiming one's consciousness toward a specific goal. Our Rabbis taught that a person must direct his prayers to heaven,[2] so that prayer is a guided ascent of the mind to Hashem.

Complete Concentration

The world must cease to exist in the mind of one who is about to pray.[3] Because *kavanah* binds us to the Divine, it is essential that the worshipper's entire existence be absorbed in the action of *tefillah*. We must strive to secure this connection at all costs.[4]

In fact, concentration during *tefillah*, especially during the *Amidah* prayer, must be so complete that "even if a king greets him he should not answer him."[5]

A Jewish man was once on a journey when he realized that it was time to say his prayers. Because there was no synagogue nearby, he moved to the side of the road and began to pray.

When he reached the Shemoneh Esrei, a Roman nobleman passed by. The prince was used to being greeted respectfully by everyone. His subjects were afraid of him, for they knew that if they did not react reverently they would be punished.

The Roman saw the Jewish man standing in the field, engrossed in his prayers. He was saying the Shemoneh Esrei so intently that he did not even look up. The prince called out a greeting, but the man did not answer. The prince grew angrier with every passing minute. When the Jew finally finished, the prince shouted, "Fool! Do you not see who is passing by? How dare you not greet me! If I had stabbed you with my sword, who would have saved you?"

"Please," pleaded the G-d fearing man. "Perhaps if I explain what I was doing, you will not be angry. Tell me, Your Highness, have you ever stood before the king?"

"Certainly," answered the nobleman proudly. "I have stood before the king many times!"

"If a simple man, or even another prince, were to greet you while you were in the presence of the king, would you stop to answer him?" the Jew asked.

"Of course not!" answered the Roman. "It is forbidden to speak to anyone while standing before the king. This would be a grave insult to His Majesty!"

"What would the king do to you if you interrupted your audience with him to greet someone?"

"He would kill me!"

"I was standing in prayer before the King of all kings," the Jew explained. "How could I stop to greet you?"

The Roman thought for a moment. "You are right!" he said. He now understood why the man had not greeted him, and he was no longer angry. He allowed the Jew to continue his journey in peace. (Koh Asu Chachameinu)

A Rabbi was once praying when a poisonous snake crawled over his legs. His disciples could not believe that he had felt nothing. He hadn't even noticed that a snake had come near him. (Berachos 34)

A person standing in prayer should feel that he stands alone with Hashem. The verse, "No man shall go with you. No man shall be seen upon that mountain," *(Shemos 34,3)* is the key to this approach. In the entire world only the individual and G–d exist. Then there can be no distractions. Nothing can disturb such a *tefillah*.[6]

Every Rosh Hashanah the Sanzer Rav would lead the prayers in the town's largest shul. His heartrending prayers penetrated to the highest realms. His ardor was so intense that he never noticed what was happening around him. There were times that he would take hold of a hot stove and not feel it burning him.

One Rosh Hashanah the shul was so crowded that a great number of men climbed on the roof to daven there. Suddenly the roof above the women's section began to buckle. People fled the building. The Rebbe continued to daven with such fervor that he did not notice the noise or the panic. Finally, someone pulled him to safety through a window.

All the way home, the Sanzer Rebbe said nothing. He went straight to his own shul and continued davening. Hearing his voice uplifted in prayer, many people joined him and continued davening with him. Only after Musaf did the Rebbe wonder why they had fled the large shul earlier. (The Sanzer Rav)

When Reb Dovid Feinstein was hired by a gentile he stipulated that he be granted time off from work each day to recite the daily tefillos. The gentile agreed, but soon regretted his concession. Reb Dovid would recite his prayers carefully and with intense concentration; as far as the employer was concerned, he took far more time than was necessary.

One day the employer decided to teach his Jew a lesson. He positioned himself behind the praying Reb Dovid, aimed his gun and pulled the trigger. A bullet whizzed above Reb Dovid's *head. The gentile expected to see the Jew collapse in fright. He was greatly disappointed to see him continue praying as if nothing had occurred. When he saw how intensely Reb Dovid prayed, the gentile realized that he was truly a G–d fearing man. Never again did he complain about the length of the Jew's prayers. (Reb Moshe)*

Our concentration on our prayers should be similar to that of a person listening to a story that is so absorbing that he doesn't want to miss a word. He is totally unconscious of his surroundings. The story is so enthralling that he is oblivious to hunger, thirst, cold or heat. All his senses are engrossed in the continuing saga.

When the words of prayer have a comparable effect on us, they are so enjoyable that our senses immediately seek to converge on and delight in them, becoming submerged in their radiance. "Calling out to Hashem in truth" *(Tehillim 145)* includes the effort to subsume ourselves into the words of prayer.

The Soul of Our Prayers

The words of prayer are like the skin of a fruit, while the thoughts that accompany prayer are the fruit itself. When a person prays with his tongue alone, with his mind drifting off to other matters, the prayer is like a skin without the fruit, a body without the soul. Regarding such a person, the Torah states, "Because this nation has approached Me, honoring Me with their mouths and lips, but their heart was far from Me, and their fear of Me was by force of habit." *(Yeshayahu 29,13)* The severity of their punishment is great.[7]

"My soul yearns, indeed it pines, for the courtyards of Hashem. My heart and my flesh will sing joyously to the Living G–d. Even the bird found a home and the free one, a nest for herself, when she laid her young by Your altars." *(Tehillim 84,3-5)* If heart and flesh are not united in song, we are no better than the bird that finds a home in the Temple. It too chirps and sings in holy places. Only *kavanah* makes our hymn unequalled.[8]

When a person enters *shul*, Hashem and the angels shower him with blessing. If his prayer turns out to be mindless prattle, the angels call out, "Is this the man whose prayers we waited for? Is this the man we blessed?"[9]

Davening with *kavanah* preserves a person's wisdom.[10] Those who simply babble the words of prayer end up prattling away their wisdom. Based on the principle of "measure for measure," one who *davens* mindlessly foregoes the wisdom of his mind.[11]

We forfeit this world and the world to come when we pray with our soul in sleep mode. When matters of the spirit must be attended to, body and soul must be summoned to perform zealously. Praying with true kavanah is worth the effort, for if we pray with proper intention even once, this prayer will elevate all the accumulated prayers which had been said without *kavanah*.[12]

"Those who say the morning prayers and the evening *Shema* with *kavanah* are guaranteed a successful day." *(Yaaros Devash*

Derush 4) When a person prays the entire *Amidah* prayer with heartfelt devotion, eighteen hundred angels receive his prayer. He is saved from *Gehinnom* and will enter *Gan Eden*.[13]

Learning from Chizkiyahu

When Yeshayahu came to Chizkiyahu and told him that he was dying, and that there was no possibility of doing *teshuvah*, Chizkiyahu refused to accept the finality of the decree. He refused to give up hope, even when the prognosis came from the Almighty Himself. He said, "Son of Amotz, finish your prophecy and leave. Thus have I received from the house of my father's father, 'Even if a sharp sword lies on a person's neck, he should not despair from [receiving Hashem's] mercy.'" *(Melachim II 20,2)*

The verse then tells us, "He turned his face to the wall and prayed to Hashem, and Chizkiyahu cried an intense cry." *(Melachim II 20,3)* Chizkiyah *davened* from the depth of his heart, with the complete knowledge that Hashem could help him. Hashem immediately acknowledged Chizkiyahu's heartfelt words and granted him fifteen more years of life. Before Yeshayahu had even left the inner courtyard of Chizkiyahu's palace, he was instructed to return and tell Chizkiyahu, "I have heard your prayer. I have seen your tears. Behold, I am healing you. On the third day you shall go up to the house of Hashem." *(Melachim II 20,4-5)*[14] His prayers have become the prototype for prayer from the heart.[15]

R' Chaim Shmulevitz tried to persuade the Tchebiner Rav, Rabbi Dov Berish Wiedenfeld, to attend an important meeting of the leading rabbis of Agudas Yisrael. Rabbi Wiedenfeld refused but would not say why. When R' Chaim continued to plead with him to join them, for it was a matter of great importance for the Jewish people, he persisted in his refusal. Finally he told R' Chaim that thirteen years earlier he had been dangerously ill and, like Chizkiyahu, he had turned his face to the wall and requested another fifteen years of life, promising to dedicate himself to the study of Torah. His prayer was accepted. Since then, he had refused to get involved in anything but the study of Torah. (Marbitzei Torah MeOlam HaChassidus)

The Power of Kavanah

The more devout our prayer, the greater and more wondrous its effect. Quantity is not important. It is quality that counts. Five or six chapters of *Tehillim* said with *kavanah* are very valuable. *Shema*, *bentching* and *berachos* should be said with devotion and joy. These moments of intimate communication are the building blocks of our eternal abode.[16]

Although many pray, only select individuals are heard, as the verse says, "And you [plural] shall serve Hashem your G–d, and He will bless your [singular] bread and water." *(Shemos 23,25)*[17] A request of the lips without *kavanah* may fulfill the *halachic* obligation to pray, but our heart's desire will not be granted. Hashem does not respond to those who pray without *kavanah*. He will not do what we have requested until we pray with *kavanah*.

Hashem only responds to heartfelt prayers, where the mouth and heart are as one.[18]

The *Gemara* discusses the parallel cases of two people who contract the same illness and two people who are condemned to death for the same crime. One leaves his sickbed and the other does not; one is saved and the other is executed. Why? Because one prayed with all his heart and was answered, the other did not.[19]

Prayer is a gift from Hashem. The effects of prayer are unbelievable. Deep down in man lies a great treasure of purity and light, which is released by prayer with *kavanah*. "As the flame clothes the black sooty lump of coal in a garment of fire and releases the heat imprisoned therein, so does prayer clothe a man in a garments of holiness, freeing the light and fire implanted within him by his Maker. This light then illuminates his whole being, and unites the lower and the higher worlds." *(Zohar)*

Prayer enables the person who is praying to receive what he has prayed for. It affects the quality of light, the quantity of food and water. It sustains the world and enables the world to be judged favorably. The more heartfelt our prayers, the more compassion the world receives. If we succeed in *davening* at a fervent pitch, every entity in the universe benefits. Who knows how many sick people would get better if we improve our *davening*, even if we don't daven for them specifically.[20]

R' Lazer Dovid Berlin would study and daven with intense concentration. Once the Turks were looking for him to draft him into the army. With his picture in hand, they entered the Bais Midrash where he was studying. They searched everywhere: in the closets, in the basement and in the attic. They combed the yard, including the cistern. Their search was painstaking, but they never even saw him.

Many years later the British broke into his house in the wee hours of the morning, looking for illegal weapons. They began to throw all the seforim to the ground. Rebbetzin Berlin slipped out and ran to shul for her husband. When he arrived in his tallis and tefillin, he sat on his chair and continued with his prayers in the same heartfelt manner in which he always prayed, oblivious to what was happening around him.

When the British soldiers saw R' Lazer Dovid, the ruthless look on their faces was replaced by awe. Pointing to the books, they asked if they were Bibles, then humbly nodded and left. The family saw clearly the manifestation of the verse, "The nations of the world will see the name of Hashem upon you and they will fear you." (See Berachos 6; Sippurim Yerushalmiyim)

When R' Chaim Shmulevitz was asked to eulogize R' Elya Lapian, he announced that it was impossible to eulogize a person who had been considered exceptionally righteous three generations ago. He maintained that there was no one in our generation who was capable of relating to R' Elya.

However, he felt compelled to repeat one anecdote about R' Elya's life which involved him. "Eight years ago I was dangerously ill. Do you know who saved my life? It was R' Elya and his prayers. I can't reveal the details, but I know for a fact that it was his prayers that saved me. I never had a chance to thank him, so I am doing so now."

When the Mashgiach of Kaminetz heard this, he took it upon himself to uncover the details. R' Chaim's vocal cords had become paralyzed. The doctor told him that nothing could be done. He then went to R' Elya to ask for advice. R' Elya replied that he could not imagine that Hashem would prevent R' Chaim from delivering his lectures. "You still have so much Torah and mussar to transmit to others!"

R' Elya asked for R' Chaim's mother's name and promised to pray on his behalf. A short time later he returned to the doctor, only to be told that his condition had dramatically improved. The doctor could not believe that it was the same person he had examined a few days before. From that point on R' Chaim began to lecture in mussar in addition to his regular Torah lecture. (HaMashgiach MiKaminetz)

Acceptable Prayer

Through the power of prayer, even the simplest man can converse with Hashem. Every hour can be the hour of prayer, every field and forest may be a dwelling for Hashem. When a person prays with passion and sincerity, it is the prayer that makes him worthy of receiving his request. Through the very act of praying, man demonstrates that he has arrived at the realization that only Hashem can grant his plea, even if he is devoid of all other merit.[21]

> *The Yalkut on Melachim II 21 discusses the repentance of Menashe. He was taken prisoner, placed in a copper pot with small holes and a fire was lit below him. In his anguish he appealed to all the idols in the world to save him. Receiving no response, he recalled his father's teaching that when tragedy strikes it is possible to return to Hashem. Menashe then cried out to Hashem, "If You save me, then all will be well. If You don't, then I will know that all gods are equal."*

> *The angels attempted to prevent his prayers from reaching Hashem. They said, "Master of the Universe, is it possible to forgive a man who set up an idol in the Sanctuary?" Hashem replied that if He did not accept his repentance, He would be closing the door to all penitents. What did Hashem do? He created a tunnel under the heavenly throne for Menashe's prayers to rise before Him.*

This *Midrash* is difficult to understand. How would Hashem's refusal to heed Menashe's prayers be an indication that all powers are equal? Theoretically, it was only logical that the idols he had worshipped all his life should have responded to his cries. Their silence, therefore, testified to their worthlessness. Yet why should Hashem have responded to his call? All his life Menashe had killed the servants of Hashem, filling Yerushalayim with blood, contemptuously calling out to Hashem as the very last resort. It would have been legitimate for Hashem to ignore him.

Yet Hashem responded even to Menashe's appeal. Hashem is different from all other powers, because His compassion is without constraint and is boundless. If we call out to Hashem from the depths of vice and iniquity, Hashem will respond and accept our repentance. Menashe correctly counted on Hashem's unrestricted compassion, and his life was saved.[22]

Prayer from the Heart

Each of our two hundred and forty-eight organs is designated for a mitzvah. *Tefillah* is assigned to the heart. Prayer that comes from the lips only, and not from the heart, may fulfill the requirement of prayer, but does not command the same response.[24] True and effective prayer results from the totality of heart and lips.[25]

The *Gemara* informs us that the G–d of Avraham will help whoever establishes a set place for his prayers.[26] This set place refers to the mouth, ears and heart. When all three function in unison, authentic prayer results.[27]

The *Rosh* writes that one must *daven* from the heart like a son having a heart-to-heart talk with his father.[28] If the son were to speak to his father with his attention elsewhere, the father would get very angry. How much more careful must we be to express ourselves with heartfelt earnestness when we are speaking to the King of kings! It is not the words of prayer that rise to Hashem; it is the burning desire of our hearts that rises like smoke toward heaven.[29]

Those who heard the prayers of R' Aharon Kohen, Rosh Yeshiva of Chevron, were convinced that they heard his soul singing. It seemed to them that they could hear the loftier elements of his soul striving to rise to its source.

As he davened he would knock his hand on his shtender for emphasis. He knocked so hard that his hands would start to bleed, but he never noticed. (Moreshes Avos)

Prayer is a complete unconditional surrender of the self to Hashem. If the mind is not fully preoccupied with prayer, the bond is loose and incomplete, leaving man exposed to the danger of extraneous thoughts intruding on his prayer. Even thoughts of Torah and *mitzvos* must be avoided.[30]

Man's mind darts from thought to thought and from place to place, particularly during prayer. The service of the heart is the effort to prevent our thoughts from straying and remain focused on the words in our *siddur*.[31]

The author of *Chovos HaLevavos* gives his own comprehensive definition of this concept. "When involving yourself with duties which require both body and heart, such as praying before G–d, Blessed be He, remove from your heart any thoughts which might distract you from your prayers. Then, you must contemplate to Whom your *tefillos* are being directed, what it is you hope to derive from them, and the words and concepts that you will express."

We conclude the *Shemoneh Esrei* with Dovid HaMelech's entreaty, "May the expressions of my mouth and the meditations of my heart find favor before You, Hashem, my Rock and my Redeemer." *(Tehillim 19,15)* The *Chovos HaLevavos* warns us that it is a great disgrace to claim to have spoken to G–d with his heart, when one's heart was actually absent from his prayers.[32]

R' Zadok HaKohen of Lublin interprets these words as a plea to accept the meditation of the heart just completed, even if it happened to be adulterated with fantasies and alien thoughts, since Hashem is the Rock of our heart and the source of all our thoughts. "My redeemer" refers to the redemption of the truth from the fantasies in which it is entangled.[33]

Because distracting thoughts overcome us during prayer, we should recite these concluding word slowly and deliberately, with concentration. It should be our final attempt to ensure that our prayers will be answered favorably. One should not rush away immediately after ending one's prayers so as not to give the impression that praying is a burdensome task.[34]

Yaakov granted Yosef the city of Shechem in addition to the portion of the land he received with his brothers, as a reward for arranging Yaakov's burial in Eretz Yisrael. Yaakov told Yosef that he took Shechem from the hands of the Emorites when he helped Shimon and Levi defend themselves. Yaakov said, "I have given you a greater portion than your brothers, a portion that I have taken from the Emori with my sword and my bow." (Bereishis 48:22) The Mechilta asks: Did he conquer it with his sword and bow? He conquered it with prayer.

Why doesn't the verse specifically state that "sword and bow" denotes prayer? The Torah wishes to teach us that prayer is our weapon in all spiritual and physical battles. The ultimate weapon for overpowering our enemies is imploring our Creator to alleviate our anguish.[35]

The Kotzker Rebbe points out the similarity between a bow and arrow and prayer. The more you draw the bow close to yourself, the higher and further away the arrow will fly. The more you draw the prayers closer and deeper into your heart, the higher towards heaven your prayers will ascend.

Saying Blessings Carefully

Berachos were implemented to give us the opportunity to observe and grasp the wonders of creation. The *Kuzari* writes about the benefit of *berachos*, "They are instrumental in helping us take notice of life's many pleasures, to be aware of them in our heart and soul. A person should take to heart the meaning of each and every blessing and understand its intention and significance. One who does not do so does not enjoy life like a human being, but rather like an animal or a baby." *(Maamar 3,15)*

Hashem has surrounded us with countless benefits. Berachos help train us to be aware of the precious gifts He has given us. When saying any blessing on food or on a *mitzvah*, we should be overcome with gratitude to Hashem for having given us that food or commanding us to do that *mitzvah*. We should not anger

Hashem by saying the words without any thought at all.[36]

When R' Yosef Kadish Kreshevsky would shout "Amen" one could actually see the word fill up his very being, as he jumped for joy and his face lit up with bliss. When others said berachos, his eyes would light up like an elderly man who has been informed of the birth of his first child. (Yosef Kadisha)

A man was about to slaughter a chicken on a street in the Bais Yisrael neighborhood. Before he could begin, a voice called out, "Say your beracha loudly so I can answer Amen. It has been a long time since I heard a beracha on shechitah."

When the slaughterer saw that the voice belonged to R' Yehuda Tzedaka, he immediately honored him with the second blessing said on covering the blood. R' Yehuda insisted that the beracha belonged to the slaughterer. But when the slaughterer insisted that it was his privilege to offer R' Yehuda the blessing, he did not continue to refuse.

After the chicken was slaughtered and the knife and innards checked, R' Yehuda took some earth and covered the blood. With great enthusiasm he uttered the blessing said on the covering of blood with earth. The man had never seen anyone say a blessing with such enthusiasm. R' Yehuda was so grateful for the privilege that he showered blessings on the shochet before continuing on his way.

A young man came to see R' Yehuda to get his signature on a recommendation for a position teaching Torah. Instead of orally testing the man as was usually done, he offered him a cup of tea. He then listened carefully to his beracha. When he saw that his blessing was said without the proper intent, he refused to sign the recommendation.

When R' Yehuda's two eldest sons reached Bar Mitzvah age, he was overjoyed that he could now bentch mezuman with his children. (VeZos LeYehuda)

When R' Shlomo Zalmen Auerbach was asked what extra observance one should assume during a time of crisis, he recommended being more careful about saying berachos with kavanah. To one person who asked for advice on strengthening his spirituality, he said that he himself was trying to increase his kavanah in prayer and saying blessings. He never tired of urging those around him to work on their kavanah. (Halichos Shlomo)

[1] Avudraham, page 9

[2] Tehilim 10,17

[3] Igeres Ha'Ramban

[4] Avudraham

[5] Berachos 30b

[6] Ben Poras Yosef 88d

[7] Chovos HaLevavos, Shaar Cheshbon HaNefesh 3,9; Likutei Torah Bamidbar

[8] Toldos Adam

[9] Or Yahel Part III, Parshas Vayikra, pp 144-145

[10] Sefer Ha'Chassidim chapter 46

[11] Tochachas Chayim Parshas Ekev; Yesh Nochalim chapter one

[12] Lashon Hasidim Tefillah, 51 in the name of R' Yaakov Yosef of Polenoye; Chayei Olam, chapters 64-66

[13] Siddur Ha'Rokeach 367

[14] Berachos 10

[15] Vayikra Rabbah 26,9: Devarim Rabbah

[16] Yaaros Devash, Derush 3

[17] Gra

[18] Baal HaTurim, Shemos 5,9

[19] Rosh Hashanah 18 with Rashi

[20] Leket Divrei Chizuk of R' Aharon Leib Shteinman

[21] Sefer HaIkarim, Part IV, chapter 18

[22] Ibid, chapter 16; Shearim BeTefillah, Kriah

[23] Taanis 2,2

[24] Baal HaTurim, Shemos 5,9

[25] Tosefta, Berachos 3,6; Midrash Lekach Tov adloc; Nefesh HaChaim 2:1; Sichos HaRan 75

[26] Berachos 6

[27] Ollelos Ephraim Part IV, page 2; Ben Yehoyada on Berachos

[28] Orchos Chaim 36

[29] Or HaMeir 3,16

30 Told by the Maggid to the Bais Yosef

31 Ramban on Shir HaShirim

32 Chovos HaLevavos, Shaar Cheshbon HaNefesh

33 Tzidkas HaTzaddik, 209

34 Orach Chaim 93:1

35 Birchas Peretz, Shemos

36 Sefer Chassidim cited by the Mishnah Berurah

Inner Focus

The Importance of Distraction Free Prayer

Imagine the scene: a man is having an audience with the king. In the course of his conversation with His Majesty, he throws in a few sentences on unrelated topics. The enraged king would have his head! Dare we take this approach with the King of kings?[1]

A person turns to Hashem in prayer. Yet while he speaks, he is thinking of other things. The result: Hashem will certainly ignore him.

Some people stand in prayer, and for all they know they might be reading the book of *Iyov!* Meanwhile, their eyes are wandering; they are making statements with their facial expressions, adding emphasis with their fingers. They may be curiously observing what their neighbors are doing, or listening to what everyone is saying. To top it off, they hurriedly end their prayers so they can make their own contribution. Is it any surprise that this type of behavior greatly angers Hashem?[2]

At the end of *Shemoneh Esrei* we say, "Let the words of my prayers be desirable to You, and, also, the thoughts of my heart, which I cannot express, be desirable in front of You." How can someone not be ashamed to say these words at the end of *Shemoneh Esrei*, if he has no recollection of having actually said the words of the prayer? He is unsure if he has said all nineteen blessings of *Shemoneh Esrei*.

Unfortunately, people rely on their mouths to say what it has been trained to say. Someone who prays in this way can be compared to servants of a king who chop the wood, draw the water, slaughter the animals, skin them, light the fire and prepare the pots. Yet in the end, they bring the king empty pots – because they never bothered to cook the food. They failed to understand that the other preparations are of no value without the final step.

R' Elya Lapian told of a trip with a horse and wagon. Suddenly the driver let the reins drop and prepared to take a nap. When R' Elya asked him what he was doing, he replied that there was nothing to worry about, for the horse knew the route very well. He could get to the destination with no help from his master. And so it was. The horse stopped only when he reached the spot where his master always gave him something to drink.

The experience reminded R' Elya of the prayers of the person who prays with no conscious intention. Just like the horse, he knows the verbal route well. He knows where to stop, where to continue, where to bow and where to stand upright. Woe to that person! The shame of such prayer is too great to bear. (Lev Eliyahu)

R' Shlomo Zalmen Auerbach wondered if mindless prat-
tling with a siddur in hand was any better than talking in one's
sleep. He was uncertain whether such invocations even qualify
as prayer.

Empty Words Anger Hashem

We are warned not to pray as if we are reading a letter,[4] or
digging in the ground or chopping wood.[5] A person who *davens*
with his mind elsewhere is like a servant whose master is coming
for a visit. The servant instructs his wife and children to honor the
master and attend to his every need. But then the servant ignores
his master and goes off to engage in some frivolous activity. He
does not honor him personally in any way. Naturally, the master
is angered, and he turns on his servant. Instead of accepting the
honor and comfort offered him by the wife and children, the
master throws everything in the servant's face.[6]

When we are praying but not concentrating, we are like that
servant. True, our limbs are vibrating, our mouths are mumbling
words; but our real selves are far away, taking care of our affairs.
It is impossible to comprehend the gravity of this behavior.[7]

R' Yerucham, the Mashgiach of Mir, used to say that *tefilah*
without proper intention is like putting *tefillin* around the neck —
such behavior disgraces the *mitzvah*.[8]

Rabbi Levi Yitzchak of Berditchev greeted several men in
the synagogue after they had finished their prayer. His warm

greeting, appropriate to someone who had just returned from a distant place, aroused the interest and wonder of the entire congregation. R' Levi Yitzchak found it necessary to explain. "In their minds, these men were wandering around the markets and fairs during prayer, selling their goods. Their thoughts returned here to the synagogue when they had finished praying. I thought it was only appropriate to greet them as newcomers should be greeted." (Toldos Kedushas Levi)

The utterances of the tongue should correspond to the thoughts of the mind. One should not utter his *tefillos* mechanically and habitually, like a parrot; each word should be accompanied with the proper thoughts and intent before Hashem.[9] If we simply mouth the words of prayer without feeling that we are addressing Hashem, we end up speaking only to ourselves! On the other hand, if a person mentally requests that Hashem forgive him, and does not verbalize his thoughts, he is forgiven. It is the thought that counts.[10]

There was once a manager who had been appointed to oversee the work of the employees in a factory. While the company owner was away, he was responsible for insuring that everything functioned smoothly. All employees were asked to report to the manager's office daily and listen as the manager read aloud the instructions left behind by the boss. He carefully uttered each word just as the owner had ordered, and did an impeccable job of delivering the instructions.

When the boss returned, he was shocked to see the condition of his factory. Machines were broken and workers stood around idle. He angrily asked the manager for an explanation.

"Did you follow the instructions I left behind with you?"

"Why, of course!" the manager defended himself. "I read them to all of the workers every day while you were gone."

"Now I know why there is such a mess!" the boss said in exasperation. "You read the instructions, but you didn't bother to see that they were carried out. Do you think I left them for you to read them every day? Reading will not achieve the goal!" (Lishmor VeLaasos pages 31-32)

When we are told to serve Hashem with all our hearts, this means devoting our *entire* heart, our total concentration. to our prayers, not half for Hashem and half elsewhere.[11]

Granted, this is not a simple matter. We must struggle to focus. Distracting thoughts bombard us: a business concern, a family problem, the sight of a friend, or even a word of prayer itself can send our thoughts on a tangent, bringing on an extended reverie. Our task, then, is to attempt to concentrate, to keep our minds and hearts directed toward the Creator.

On one occasion, the holy Yismach Moshe went to Lublin for Shabbos. He prayed with the Rebbe, the Chozeh of Lublin, and his chassidim. When they came to the prayer, "The soul of every living creature blesses Thy name, O Lord..." a prayer that we are obliged to pray especially earnestly, since it is during this prayer that we change our Sabbath-night soul for our day soul, it suddenly occurred to the holy Yismach Moshe that he had forgotten the key to the cupboard in his room at the inn where he had some money. This was no ordinary money: the money in that cupboard had been collected on his way to Lublin, for poor families in need. Supposing somebody was to notice the key in the lock, open the cupboard and steal the money?

It was in vain that he kept telling himself that nobody at Lublin would be such a villain as to steal on the holy Shabbos. He kept envisioning the key sticking out of the lock in the cupboard door. He was quite unable to concentrate on prayer.

Finally, he realized that these thoughts were a snare laid by the evil inclination, as a way of tempting him away from his devotions. So the holy Yismach Moshe took a stern grip on himself and started praying fervently. He thought no more of the key.

After the service, as the chassidim were sitting at the table with the Saint of Lublin, the Chozeh suddenly turned to the holy Yismach Moshe. "What's come over you, Reb Moshe? Until we reached the prayer 'The soul of every living creature,' I saw your soul going with us in our devotion. Then it got lost, and I didn't see it again until we got to Yoitzer Or. Can one allow oneself to be so distressed over forgetting a key?"
(Introduction to Yismach Moshe)

A Double-Edged Sword

The verses between *Baruch Sheamar* and *Yishtabach* are

called *Pisukei Dezimra*, verses of *zimra*. The Kabbalists define *zimra* as a pruning knife. These prayers are empowered to act as a knife, cutting away at the mental and spiritual hindrances to prayer, and decapitating all prosecuting angels.

A man brandishing a sword holds the blunt side in his hand and uses the sharp edge against his enemies. More care is required when a sword has sharp edges on both sides. Although it enables a soldier to kill more of the enemy, he is also likely to kill himself!

Prayer has been likened to a double-edged sword, for if the supplicant is not focused, his stray thoughts can rebound and inflict heavy damage, G–d forbid.[12] Instead of decapitating the powers of impurity, we enable them to gain the upper hand. Instead of enhancing Hashem's glory, we detract from it. The harmful forces resulting from the desecration of Hashem's name prevent our prayer from rising to Heaven.

A person who makes no effort to *daven* with *kavanah* is considered wicked and worthless.[13] The *Gemara* recommends that a person who does not say *Shema* with *kavanah* should be beaten, to teach him the importance of focusing on each word.[14] Why the *Shema* prayer specifically? Because the words of *Shema* describe Hashem's wrath when man does not serve Him with his whole heart. How is it that this oft-repeated warning of chastisement does not move us to higher levels of concentration?[15]

Consider the person who thinks of his business while he is *davening*. As he stands in prayer before Hashem, his mind is on his gold and silver. It is a clear indication that he does not really believe that the *Shechinah* is opposite him. To him almost applies the warning of "do not make images of gold and silver of Hashem."[16]

In his old age, R' Yechezkel of Shinova moved to Eretz Yisrael. He was given a money order to cover his expenses. He was disturbed to find that the bank note was interfering with his prayers. It lessened his trust in Hashem; it was almost as if the banknote was calling out to him, "Trust in me!" He proceeded to burn the money order, feeling that he was fulfilling the command to destroy idols. After it was destroyed, he returned to his prayers with total concentration (Rabenu HaKadosh MiShinova).

Rabbi Ruderman asked R' Moshe Shimon Zivetz why he had sent him fifty dollars (a huge sum in those days) after receiving a copy of his sefer. Rabbi Zivetz explained that his congregation had given him a large amount of money in the form of a retirement fund. Although the Rav felt very uncomfortable with the gift, he took the check and deposited it in his savings account. But he continued to be plagued with doubts. Should he leave the money in his savings account, or should he invest it in some high-dividend venture? Perhaps he ought to purchase gold or silver, which would surely increase in value?

His thoughts were so tied up with his money that he found that he could no longer daven with kavanah. He would begin

Shemoneh Esrei, and soon his mind was on how to invest his capital. This happened many times. Finally, he decided that as long as he possessed the funds, he would not be able to overcome this problem. He determined to give the money away so he could once again daven properly.

The money couldn't be returned. Instead, he began giving it to charity. He gave generously to rosh yeshivas, poor brides, and scholars like Rabbi Ruderman. He was then able to daven with a clear mind. (More Shabbos Stories, Vayechi)

Seizing the Moment

Although the *Gemara* requires that a person wait for a calm moment before beginning his prayers, we do not follow this recommendation, because we do not assume that we will *daven* properly even under the best of circumstances.[17]

Further on, the *Tur* cites the *Gemara (Berachos 34)* which requires that one repeat the first blessing of the *Amidah* if he has not said it with proper concentration. However, the *halacha* has been determined otherwise. Because we are not sure that the blessing will be any better the second time around, we do not repeat it.[18]

Nevertheless, even though we do not repeat our prayers when we realize that our minds were elsewhere, we are duty bound to acknowledge that such prayer is not worthy of the name. Uttering the words without the mind's participation is a corruption of the meaning of prayer.

Still, there is one purpose to such mindless verbiage: it allows us to preserve our link to *tefillah*.[19]

> *Someone once asked the Chofetz Chaim whether it wouldn't be better to wait until one was inspired, rather than to constantly say the prayers without kavanah.*

> *The Chofetz Chaim answered with a parable: Many towns and villages could not afford their own watchmaker, and so a travelling repairman would go from one small village to another over the course of years. People would put their broken watches aside in anticipation of his visit.*

> *When the repairman arrived, he immediately sat down to sort through the broken watches. He divided the watches into two piles: one for those that he could repair, and another for those which could not be repaired. Several watches would inevitably be beyond repair, because they had lain in a drawer and become rusted. By contrast, the watches that had been regularly wound by their owners could readily be repaired.*

> *The Chofetz Chaim pointed out that if you daven three times a day, even if you pray without kavanah, at least the davening tools are well oiled. When inspired, you will be able to daven with kavanah. However, a person who does not daven loses the habit and will be unable to daven easily even when inspired.*

Our situation in prayer is the same. We are informed that a person cannot prevent his thoughts from straying.[20] All sorts of thoughts lay claim to our minds, seizing and snatching our attention and diverting us – but at least let us work on achieving concentrated moments of prayer, free of distraction.

A woman once took some baskets of apples to the market to sell. Some mischievous children overturned her baskets, scattering the apples. She stood there, horrified, watching as the children grabbed as many apples as they could and ran off. Finally a passerby remarked, "Why don't you seize some of the apples yourself?" (Chofetz Chaim)

The onus is on us to make a concentrated effort to *daven* with *kavanah*, at the very least during certain prayers and certain blessings. R' Yosef Zundel of Salant put it this way (in the name of the *Gra*): "If your *yetzer hara* catches you (distracts you) in the blessing *Selach Lanu*, then you catch him in the blessing *Re'eh Na* (overcome him with your concentration)."[21]

A *chassid* once complained to the Piasetzna Rebbe that he could not sustain those elevated moments of worship that are the highlights of the prayers. The Rebbe explained that such exalted moments of prayer never last. Invariably, there are high and low periods. When a person never finds himself in the depths, it is an indication that he has never scaled the heights.

Whoever focuses on the fact that his prayers are often uninspiring will eventually despair, and despair is the precursor to a serious downfall.[22] A person should remain steadfast. His service is then likened to that of the foot soldier who serves the king faithfully, despite the fact that he has no access to him. His goal is to somehow get closer to the King and catch a glimpse of him, perhaps through a crack or crevice. These low periods then become the stepping stone to inspired moments of prayer.[23]

The reward for *mitzvos* is determined by the pains that we take to do what is required. We get a greater reward for going to *shul* in a storm when the ground is muddy and the weather is cold. Because it takes a concerted effort to focus on our prayers, our reward will be commensurately greater.

A wise person relishes the more difficult *mitzvos*. He is like the warrior who is looking for a battle in which he will be able to demonstrate his prowess and his love and devotion to the king.[24]

When someone confided to Rebbe Nachman that he had difficulty speaking to Hashem in prayer, he told him the following parable:

> *A great general had to surmount a mighty wall in battle. When he came to the gate, he found it blocked with a spider's web. Could you imagine anything more foolish than returning in defeat because a spider's web is blocking your path? (Sichos HaRan 232)*

We should not be discouraged by our flights of fancy, for they demonstrate how important prayer is. The *yetzer hara* knows the prodigious ramifications of prayer; he seeks to sabotage our efforts at all costs. His main ammunition is aimed at our prayers for one very important reason: by interfering with our prayers, he has destroyed our link with Hashem.[25]

Like a good soldier, one must get on with the task at hand. Though a person may not be successful in praying the entire prayer with full concentration, he will at least wound and maim the opposition, the foreign thoughts. Eventually, if he maintains his determination, he will win the battle.[26]

A successful man with no problems to speak of may find it difficult to pray with a complete heart. When all is going well, prayers inevitably lose their intensity. When fortune smiles a person feels that nothing can change. Such an individual may not even really desire the appearance of *Mashiach*, for, he may reason, "things "couldn't be better."

Things may be going well not because of his righteousness but only because Hashem is slow to anger and forgives him. Therefore he must plead with Him lest Hashem reconsider withholding the evil. Miracles do not happen every day.[27]

The *Shaloh HaKadosh* advises the person seeking higher levels of devotion to remind himself that Hashem endowed him with all the advantages he enjoys. There are no guarantees that he will always be healthy and wealthy. In the course of our exile, traumatic events have often overturned the status quo. This realization should enable even the most well established person to pray sincerely for the coming of *Mashiach*.[28]

Heavenly Assistance

Fortunately, we are not alone in this great battle. Hashem helps those who demonstrate that they are making an effort to achieve *kavanah*.

In *Tehillim (10,17)* the verse states, "Prepare their heart." The *Bach* points out that these words imply that successful concentration is not in the hands of man. We must seek to create an environment conducive to devotion. Hashem does the rest. As is clearly stated, "Whoever comes to purify himself is assisted from Heaven."[29]

We preface the *Shemoneh Esrei* with the entreaty that our Master open our lips and help our mouths tell *(yagid)* His true praise. The *Reishis Chochmah* explains that the choice of the word "*yagid*," instead of "*yomar*" (say) or "*yedaber*" (speak), suggests that we are begging Hashem to help us pray with concentration.[30]

Our sages added these words to the *Amidah* prayer because spirituality had declined and people were finding it difficult to sustain purity of intention in prayer.[31] They also felt that we needed Hashem's help to formulate our words because our awe might make us speechless.

> *R' Eliyahu Lapian recounts the story of a laborer who used to lay roads in the capital. The king was so pleased with his work that he chose to honor him by inviting him to the palace for an audience. When the man arrived he was so overwhelmed with fright that his vocal cords froze and he remained mute for the rest of his life. This reflects the way we should react when standing before Hashem. We therefore ask*

for help right before we start this important prayer. (Lev Eliyahu, Part III)

It is clear, that without Hashem's help, *kavanah* would be impossible.[32] Knowing this, the righteous implore Hashem to listen to their *tefillos.*[33] We have already noted that the ancient pious ones would delay their prayers for at least an hour in order to direct their hearts to Hashem. The Kotzker Rebbe explains that during that hour, they were praying that they succeed in directing their hearts to their father in Heaven.[34]

The Sanzer Rav explains the words, "And I pleaded to Hashem at that time saying." *(Devarim 3,23)* We should plead with Hashem "at that time" – when we are about to pray – to help us succeed in our "saying": please enable us to say the words of prayer with enthusiasm and devotion.

A chassid asked Rabbi Chaim of Sanz, "Rebbe, what do you do before the prayers?"

Rabbi Chaim answered, "Before the prayers I pray for inspiration."

R' Shmuel Aharon Yudelevitz composed a special prayer which he said prior to his prayers, begging Hashem to ensure that his praying not be disturbed. (Meilo shel Shmuel)

There are times when we find it difficult to concentrate on our *davening.* We should not become discouraged. The *Baal Shem Tov* recommends that at times like these we should stop and *daven* to Hashem to help us *daven.*[35]

What happens to a prayer that is said with the proper intent? Angels raise this prayer to Heaven and hand it over to the angel Sandalphon, who transfers it to the Heavenly throne. 1,800 angels stand ready to receive our *tefillos*.[36] Michael is in charge of *Shacharis*, Gavriel is in charge of *Mincha* and Oriel is responsible for the *Maariv* prayer.

A prayer without the proper intent has a very different fate. These prayers do not ascend on High; they wander aimlessly through the world. Imagine the chagrin of the person who presents himself before G–d after a lifetime on this earth, only to find that he has only a paltry two or three *tefillos* credited to his account – out of thousands and thousands of recited prayers.[37]

> *Once when Reb Nosan was in Uman, he saw a certain Reb Moshe praying very fervently. Some time afterwards Reb Nosan returned to Uman and saw that Reb Moshe was no longer praying with the same intensity and effort. Reb Nosan said to him, "Reb Moshe, you've weakened. You're not praying the way you used to. Take my advice and start again. Look at me. My beard is already white, yet I still have intentions of becoming a good Jew!" (Avenecha Barzel page 63)*

Yet there is still hope for those incomplete prayers. If a person strains every nerve to maintain his devotion, he can actually elevate the many prayers that he had said without proper intent.[38]

How does this work? On *Rosh Hashanah*, Sandalphon collects these prayers for further revaluation on Yom Kippur.[39] At that point, Hashem seeks out a heartfelt *Magen Avraham*, a good *Mechaye Mesim*, a sincere *Kel Kadosh*. These sincere prayers are then used to elevate the unsatisfactory blessings which had been uttered without concentration.

But we must take the first step! The prayers that have not been elevated by our remorse are relegated to nothingness.[40]

> *While recovering from a heart attack, R' Zev Dov Chechik returned to the hospital for a check-up. The doctor examined him thoroughly and then stressed the crucial importance of strictly following all his instructions. These included taking various medicines at different times of the day, a radical change of diet, a program of exercise and other precautions. R' Zev listened attentively. On his way out of the hospital, he was overheard saying to himself, "I could have avoided all this if only I had prayed better on Rosh Hashanah." (The Commentators Siddur)*

Achieving Inner Focus

Before we can actively seek concentration and proper *kavanah* in our prayers, we must first focus our minds inwardly. And that means removing all outer distractions. How can this be done?

There is no magic formula. But our *chachamim* have suggested several ways of achieving this goal:

• The Mekubalim advise that a person who is being constantly distracted should say "*pi pi pi*" (an abbreviation for the names Palti and Yosef, two men who withstood temptation). He should then make a spitting noise with his tongue between his lips.[41]

• Running your right hand over your forehead three times is another way of removing distracting thoughts.[42]

• Run your right hand over your forehead and say the verse, "Create for me, *Elokim*, a pure heart and renew within me a rectified spirit." If distracting thoughts recur, repeat the process.[43]

• Visualization can be an aid to avoiding distracting thoughts. When distracted by irrelevant thoughts, we should visualise wicked strangers – the personification of the evil inclination – attempting to throw us into a mud - filled pit. Similarly, we should imagine that we desire to enter the palace of the King, and suddenly enemies appear blocking our way. The only possible reaction is to strengthen our resolve, forcefully resist these distracting evil beings, and throw ourselves on the mercy of Hashem, requesting His help.[44]

Finally, it may help to be inspired by other's true, distraction-free prayer.

The Vilna Gaon davened standing like a minister before the king, inspiring the listener with a fear of Hashem that lasted for a year or more.

After the Pesach Seder, everyone would leave the room and the Gra would remain alone. One year a relative hid in the room to see what would happen. The Gra started saying Shir HaShirim with such intense devotion that it seemed that his soul had left his body. The relative jumped out of his hiding place and rushed to revive him so he would not die. (HaGaon HaChassid MiVilna)

The *Chazon Ish* davened with great intensity, swept away by the very fact that he was in the antechamber of the King, privileged to be counted amongst those who serve Him.

R' Shmarya Greinman needed an immediate answer to a life and death question. When he arrived at the home of the *Chazon Ish*, he found him in the midst of his prayers, his eyes tightly closed. Because the question required an immediate answer, he approached the *Chazon Ish* and whispered the question in his ear.

When he saw that he was not reacting, he tapped the *Chazon Ish* on his arm. When the Rav still didn't react, R' Shmarya took the liberty of gently shaking the *Chazon Ish*. When he finally opened his eyes, R' Shmarya stepped back, aghast. The *Chazon Ish* looked as if he was coming back from another world. R' Shmaryah quickly asked the question; the *Chazon Ish* answered with a nod of his head, and went back to his devotions. (Told by Rabbi S. Greinman)

Rabbi Auerbach told of standing next to the *Chazon Ish* while he prayed, and seeing the tears stream down his face as he said the words, "Enlighten our eyes with Your Torah." Once when he was leading the prayers, he had to stop to contain his tears before proceeding. (Told by Rabbi S. Greinman) He prayed with such effort that he collapsed into a chair after completing his davening. (As told by Rabbi Mordechai Mann and Rabbi Baruch Yitzchak) One evening after midnight, R' Sholom Schwadron passed the *Chazon Ish's* house and saw him *praying, crying and shaking like a lulav. (from the memoirs of Rabbi Tovolesky)*

In 1946, members of the Irgun attacked a British office in Ramat-Gan. A chase ensued, with the assailants heading in the direction of Bnei Brak.

As the silent Shemoneh Esrei was being recited in the daily minyan at the Chazon Ish's home, the sounds of approaching gunfire were heard. The pursuers headed past the Chazon Ish's apartment and the stench of gunpowder filled the air. Sounds of battle mingled with screams of fright from the neighborhood residents. Everyone in the minyan was shaken-except for the Chazon Ish, whose hands calmly rested on the pillar next to him as he continued davening with perfect serenity. As someone present put it, the Chazon Ish was in conversation with his Maker, and nothing in the world could disturb his concentration. (Chazon Ish)

Such depth of feeling is difficult to achieve and sustain for long periods of time. Yet even if experienced on occasion for a short while, they remain guiding lights in our journey towards acquiring sublime levels of concentration.

[1] Shnei Luchos HaBris, Tziyon Avodah Bais

[2] Bais Tefillah, chapter 2

[3] Maharam De Lunzano

[4] Yerushalmi Berachos 4,4

[5] Moreh Nevuchim 3,21

[6] Chovos HaLevavos, Cheshbon HaNefesh 3,9

[7] Olelos Ephraim, Part IV, page 20, Lecture 498

[8] Or Yechezkel

[9] Kuzari 3,5

[10] Yesod VeShoresh HaAvodah, Gate 2, chapter 3

[11] Bais Tefillah

[12] Lev Eliyahu

[13] Akeda, Gate 28, page 18

[14] Berachos 33; Shaloh HaKadosh, page 903

[15] Reishis Chochmah, Tozaos Chaim, Letter 176

[16] Orchos Yosher

[17] Tur 98

[18] Tur, chapter 101

[19] Michtav MeEliyahu, Part IV

[20] Bava Basra 164

[21] Oros HaGra, page 30

[22] Berachos 32

[23] Derech HaMelech, Seventh day of Pesach 1931

[24] Menucha U'Kedusha

[25] Maor VeShemesh

[26] Likutei Moharan 2,122

[27] Rabbi M. Solomon, With Hearts of Faith, page 96

[28] Shaloh HaKadosh Tamid, Ner Mitzvah

[29] Yoma 38

[30] Reishis Chochmah, Letter 178

[31] Kedushas Levi, Vaeschanan

[32] Bach, Orach Chaim 98

[33] Midrash Tehillim 108,1

[34] HaSaraf MiKotzk; Bais Tefillah in the name of R' Ephraim Zalmen Margalios

[35] Last Will and Testament of the Baal Shem Tov

[36] Tur

[37] Yaaros Devash

[38] Yaaros Devash Derush 4

[39] Zohar Bereishis

[40] Ibid; Mikdash Melech on Zohar, Part II 245,2

[41] Rabbi Moshe Kordevero

[42] Shevet Musar, chapter 31

[43] Mishnah Berurah 98,2 citing the Shaloh

[44] Bais Tefillah

Mastering the Art of Prayer

Strategies to Acquire Kavanah

Without plans and strategies it is difficult to pray with proper intention.[1] It takes constant sustained efforts to pray as we were meant to. The *Kohanim* would study for five years to familiarize themselves with their responsibilities.[2] A person who does not make a concerted effort to daven with enthusiasm suffers the consequences in this world and in the world to come. At the very least, we should seek to say a small part of each tefilah with the proper devotion.[3]

A person's connection to the Divine should grow and consolidate over time. This maturation will be reflected in our prayer. A person about to complete his graduate requirements is much more accomplished than an undergraduate entering the program. A person seeking proficiency in prayer must similarly move from one level of understanding to another.

Every bit of spiritual growth will affect our prayers in a positive way; every genuine prayer will affect the measure of spirituality in our lives. A person who savors his prayer will find that the process enriches his spirit. His finer senses are honed and his faith is fortified.[4]

A person who is immersed in the study of Torah and the performance of *mitzvos* achieves greater closeness to Hashem. His love and fear of Hashem become an intrinsic part of his makeup. Because his daily activities are focused on Hashem's service, he can concentrate effortlessly on the words of prayer. This is why "the prayers of the righteous are heard" *(Mishlei 15,29)* for they readily achieve the level of *kavanah* that is required.[5]

In the minyan of R' Zerach Braverman every word of prayer was said clearly and with concentration together, aloud. Whoever heard this group say Pesukei DeZimra was inspired to repentance. When a guest joined the minyan he would inevitably ask who was sick or in trouble, believing that only a tragedy could inspire such passionate davening.

Observing R' Zerach pray was like witnessing a child in total subservience to his father. His face aflame, his body alert, he poured out his heart to his Maker. Many great men living in Yerushalayim at the turn of the last century would join the minyan so they could study this true service of Hashem.

During the week, R' Zerach would begin saying Mizmor Shir Chanukas 52 minutes before sunrise. He would don his tallis between Yishtabach and Yotzer Or. Each word was carefully enunciated with great enthusiasm. The words of Shema were uttered with emphasis on all the necessary pauses.

Right after davening, he would quickly take off his tefillin. When asked why he hurried to remove them, he explained that he didn't have the strength for protracted focus on the proper meanings and intentions of tefillin.

Nothing deterred him from praying with his usual enthusiasm. He was once traveling to a distant village with a group of Rabbis when the wagon driver got lost. With the time for prayer approaching, they stopped in the desert to pray. The other rabbis were determined to pray as quickly as possible so they could make their way back to civilization before darkness. But R' Zerach prayed slowly and with great devotion. His prayers reflected no fear or anxiety. One would have thought that he was praying in the yeshiva as usual. The people there were amazed at the way fear and danger did not distract R' Zerach's devotion at all.

People in Yerushalayim would say, "If only we could pray with such devotion on Yom Kippur as R' Zerach prays Maariv each motzaei Shabbos."

On Yom Kippur, R' Zerach's minyan would be overwhelmed with joy as they said the Neilah prayers. Their prayers continued well past the time for ending the fast. Because of the sweetness of their devotions, they felt no hunger. (BeTuv Yerushalayim)

Prior to Shabbos, the Klausenberger Rebbe had an attack of excruciating pain from kidney stones. His Rebbetzin begged him to daven at home, but the Rebbe insisted on going to shul.

The Rebbetzin finally acquiesced, suggesting that he not pray at length.

The Rebbe began his prayers with the same enthusiasm as he always did, slowly and with devotion. When he arrived at Boee LeShalom, he began to dance with great excitement. For three-quarters of an hour he danced. The chassidim who knew of their Rebbe's illness were astounded. He then said Mizmor Shir for about half an hour.

When he returned home, the Rebbetzin was waiting with only one word: "Why?" The Rebbe replied, "I don't know. As soon as I began praying, the pain passed. It looks like Boee LeShalom is a remedy for pain." (Marveh LeZameh)

Unfortunately, there is no magical formula for prayer with devotion. *Davening* without concentration is one of the three sins that a person cannot avoid,[6] but there are a number of things a person can do to increase his concentration.

Applying Music Appreciation Techniques to Prayer

The guidelines for music appreciation can be applied to the art of prayer. There are many who react instinctively to music without any proper training, just as there are people whose souls reach out naturally to Hashem and do no need to be taught how to *daven*.

For those who are unmoved by music, experts can teach them to appreciate the fine art. Listen to a piece of music in an environment with no distractions; concentrate on the various strains of the melody. Repeat this process several times and note the different themes of the arrangement. Study the background of the score. Call on an expert for help in discerning how the various strains blend together in perfect harmony, differentiating one instrument from another.

Acquiring proper devotion during *tefillah* involves a similar process. It requires total concentration in an environment with no distractions. Studying the meaning of the words of prayer and their origin enables us to concentrate on the themes of the various phrases. One should also continuously try to pray with the right *kavanah*, until one has become an earnest *davener*. Everyone is capable of achieving a heightened level of consciousness.[7]

A professional musician is a good role model for a person who does not feel like praying. If a musician were to put off practicing because he was not in the mood, it would be the end of his career. To continue practicing enables him to continue playing. Once he begins playing the melody, it is likely that he will be inspired to play with enthusiasm.[8]

Chacham Menashe Levi aroused a passion for prayer in all those who heard him pray. His son remembers accompanying his father to the Machane Yehudah market where he would walk from stall to stall, gathering the vendors together for prayer.

One of the vendors revealed that after praying with the tzaddik only once a week, he learned to love praying, particularly with a minyan. Even when the tzaddik was not praying with them, the vendor was able to maintain the same enthusiasm his presence had inspired. Many admitted that R' Menashe Levi walked them through their initial approach to prayer. Later they were able to master the art of prayer on their own. (VeAni Tefillah)

Knowing the Meaning of the Prayers

After 120 years in this world, when we stand before Hashem and are asked, "What did you have in mind when you said the various prayers? What is the meaning of this word and that word?" we will feel a searing anguish at having prayed so many times without knowing the meaning of what we were saying.

If a person does not understand what he is saying, the power of his prayers is greatly diminished. Unless we understand what we are saying, how can we be moved by prayer, which reflects the entire spectrum of Jewish experience and Jewish possibilities?

We must recite the words as if we really mean them. Sad passages should be said in an anguished voice, happy passages should be said joyously. This can only be done if we know what we are saying.

R' Yosef Chaim Sonnenfeld's prayers would so deeply affect his listeners that they would have to turn aside to overcome their emotions. One man felt that he needed some privacy to recover his equilibrium after R' Yosef Chaim led the

Mincha prayers at a wedding. He felt uncomfortable weeping when everyone was rejoicing. He found a small room where he hoped to regain his composure. To his surprise, the room was full of people trying to do the same thing. (Marah DeArah DeYisroel)

When Rabbi Shlomo Zalmen Auerbach was asked to define a good day, he replied, "A day in which I have succeeded in praying all three prayers with proper kavanah, focusing on the simple meaning of all the words. Der Baruch zoll sein a Baruch, un der Atah a Atah – the Baruch should be a Baruch and the Atah an Atah – that is a real holiday for me." (Halichos Shlomo)

Kavanah can be achieved by referring to inspirational texts prior to *davening* and reviewing *Shulchan Aruch Orach Chaim 98* at least once a week.[9] Rabbi Shmuel Houminer advises that after one has become familiar with the plain meaning of the words of prayer, he should study them in depth. This means gaining a better understanding of the deeper concepts of our relationship with Hashem. Regular study groups are conducive to this goal.[10] Many scholars wrote commentaries on prayer to help facilitate our *tefillos*, such as the *Yaarov Devash, Yesod Veshoresh Hoavodah, Otzar Hatefilah*. Seek out these texts and use them to enrich your prayers.

One should particularly study the relevant prayers before the holidays. In the late seventeenth century, Rabbi Sheftel, the son of the Shaloh HaKadosh, instituted such study groups in the community of Frankfurt.

Between Kabolas Shabbos and Maariv, R' Shlomo Zalmen Auerbach would teach his young children the meaning of the words of prayer. He set aside time to study the same topic with his wife until she mastered the meaning of the prayers. His daughters were encouraged to ensure that Biur Tefillah, studying the meanings of prayer, took precedence over any other Torah topic in their schools. (Halichos Shlomo)

When the Mashgiach of Kaminetz would lecture on the importance of prayer, the boys would daven Shemoneh Esrei with new intensity. The boys even outdid the Mashgiach himself and finished their prayers after him. (HaMashgiach MiKaminetz)

We should not be distressed if we do not fathom the awesome depth of the words of prayer like the Kabbalists. We should rather focus on the plain meaning of the words, then humbly present our prayers to Hashem and pray that they perform as they should.[11]

When Rebbe Nachman was deathly ill on the final Rosh Hashanah of his life, he asked his little grandson, Yisrael, to pray for him. "Master of the world!" Yisrael called out, "Let my grandfather be well!" The people nearby started smiling. The Rebbe said, "This is how to pray. Simply! What other way is there?" (Tzaddik 439)

There was once a great king who was beloved by his subjects. His ministers and wise men passed before the king, bearing gifts of food and all types of sweets. There was a poor man among the others who also wished to honor the king. He took stalks of wheat, washed them well and put them in a pure vessel. When it was his turn to pass before the king, he said, "My master the king, I wished to bring more food, but I did not possess the means to do so. I have brought the fruit of my labor. Please accept this offering. Form it into a final product that will please your palate and consider it my gift."

The king was pleased with his words. He used the wheat to create a delectable repast. He then appointed the man to act as his viceroy.

Focusing On the Words

Riveting one's attention on the words of prayer is an important goal of *tefillah*. The *halacha* requires that there be no obstruction between us and the wall when we *daven*. The wall represents the *Shechinah*; nothing should stand between us and Hashem's presence.[12] We must know to Whom we are speaking and what we are saying. *Kavanah* involves concentrating totally on the words of prayer, having cleared our mind of extraneous thoughts.[13] After cleansing our mind,[14] we should direct it upwards.[15]

The *Gemara* forbade praying when a person cannot concentrate on the words of prayer.[16] The *Rambam* explains that this refers to a time when a person's mind is unclear and his heart is troubled.[17] Although this *halacha* does not apply nowadays, we learn from the *Rambam's* explanation that *kavanah* involves both the head and the heart. Intellectually, we must comprehend the prayers, and emotionally, we must identify with the concepts we are expressing.

It is not easy to restrict oneself to a single thought. It takes a great deal of practice and self control to train our hearts to truly cleave to Hashem, so we will not have extraneous thoughts during prayer and can focus exclusively on the meaning of the words we are uttering. Each of us must make the effort to come up with a personal combat plan for our *milchemes mitzvah*. We must devise personal ways to focus on the words of prayer.[18]

Strain every fiber of your body to focus on the concepts inherent in every word.[19] When you say "*Baruch*," focus on Hashem as the source of all blessings. When you say "*atah*," focus on the personal relationship Hashem has with each of us. When you say Hashem's name, focus on the fact that He is Master of all, Who always was, is, and will be. When saying "*Elokeinu*," focus on Hashem's strength and His Divine Providence.

> *R' Moshe of Kobrin taught in the name of R' Mordechai of Lechovitz that whoever says the word "Lord" and at the same moment intends to say "of the world" has not said anything. When he is saying "Lord" he must devote himself entirely to the word "Lord."*

When praising Hashem, focus on the fact that Hashem alone – and no other entity – is deserving of these praises. When asking for the necessities of everyday existence, focus on the fact that only Hashem is aware of the specifics of our needs and has the ability to provide us with what we require.[20] When we ask for health, we must remember that if Hashem were to turn away from us for even a moment, G–d forbid, we would be inundated by suffering. This should enable us to rouse our heart to say the words of prayer with greater integrity.[21]

In the city of Krasna, a man announced that he would walk across the river on a tightrope if given 100 gold coins. The famous Reb Chaim of Krasna was among the spectators who came to watch. He was amazed at what a person would do for money. Yet as he stood watching the tightrope walker, Reb Chaim was impressed with the man's total concentration on his efforts. He was obviously not thinking about the 100 gold coins that he would get at the end, or he would have fallen in the water. Reb Chaim later told his students, "Imagine! If for 100 gold coins a man can concentrate so deeply on what he is doing, how much more should we concentrate when praying and serving G-d!"

The Chasam Sofer confided to his son that from the day he understood he was accountable to G-d for all his actions, he never had a stray thought during prayer. (Introduction to Siddur Chasam Sofer) The Chasam Sofer would daven leaning against the wall. His mouth would move and his face looked like a burning flame, but his body was motionless. His students kept a close eye on their Rebbe, because they worried that he would perish as a consequence of his intense prayer. (Zichron LeMoshe)

Careful Pronunciation

A person should not pray hurriedly, for he cannot properly say "*Baruch*" when the "*atah*" is impatient to get out. A person must forget his surroundings, and not be shy to linger over his prayers for fear his friends will make fun of him. He should uproot his pride and pray in a dignified manner.[22]

We should think about the translation of one or two words at a time, certainly no more than three. No more than three words should be pronounced in one breath in order to properly achieve this concentration.[23] Be careful to enunciate each word carefully.[24] Words must be uttered with the proper punctuation. Slurring distorts meanings.[25] If holy words of prayer sustain the cosmos, then mangled words of prayer ravage our universe. There are stories of great *tzaddikim* who were severely punished for the damage they caused to their spiritual environment because they were not heedful of this warning.[26]

Rav Yehudah Segal recommended pointing to every word as it is uttered.[27] One should emphasize each word as if he were counting coins.[28] R' Shimon Shkop would pray deliberately and methodically, with his eyes on the *siddur* and his finger on the place, as if he was studying the words.[29]

Eliyahu once revealed himself to a pious man. The man wondered why Eliyahu had not come before. Eliyahu replied, "It is because the chazanim and those who read from the Torah are not careful to enunciate their words properly."

"Hashem is near to those who call out to him in truth." The word emes (truth) stands for osiyos, milos, senuos – letters, words and emphasis. If one is careful about these, then his prayers will be answered and the exile will end. (Meam Loez)

R' Eliyahu Lapian would be very careful to enunciate each word properly. He would correct those who said their words improperly. Many times he would take the chazan aside and show him the places where he had uttered the word improperly. (Lev Eliyahu, biographical information)

Uttering Hashem's Name

In *Shaarei Teshuvah*, Rabbeinu Yona lists a number of sins which people do not take seriously, including mentioning the Name of G–d in vain. This sin involves transgression of the negative commandment, "You shall not take the Name of Hashem, your G–d, in vain," *(Shemos 20,1)* and the positive commandment, "Fear Hashem, your G–d." *(Devarim 10,20)* Contrary to common belief, this transgression is not limited to instances where the Name of Hashem is expressed needlessly.[30] It also refers to saying Hashem's name without concentration.[31]

Rabbi Yitzchak Chayat, author of Zera Yitzchak, tells of a friend who passed away. There was a great commotion in the court on high when he arrived. "Make way for a saint who comes to us!" the angels proclaimed. He was received with great honor.

They set a Torah scroll in his arm and asked him, "Have you fulfilled what is written here?"

"Yes," he answered.

They asked, "Who bears witness?"

Immediately angels came, those who had been created from the commandments he had fulfilled. They were beyond number, confirming his good deeds. One said, "I was created from this commandment." And so it was with all of them.

Then they asked him, "Did you take care to utter Hashem's name with devotion?" He was silent. They asked him again, but he remained silent.

They called for evidence. Bands of destructive angels clad in black came to testify. One said, "I was created on such and such a day when he pronounced the Name in prayer without due intent and concentration."

Another said, "Thus and thus it was with me." And so did all the others.

Then the members of the court on high rent their garments and said to him, "How did you not fear to pronounce His Great Name, you abject creature, without full intention? You have transgressed the commandment 'You shall not take the Name of the Lord, your G–d, in vain!'" (Exodus 20,7) The punishment was severe, but he accepted its cleansing atonement.

In *Shacharis* we say Hashem's name close to six hundred times. Every time we pronounce Hashem's name, it should be with awe and fear.[32] The *Shaloh HaKadosh* advises that we *daven* slowly and commit ourselves to pronouncing Hashem's name the correct way.[33] Using a *siddur* makes it easier to concentrate on the Name.[34] Remember: anyone who says Hashem's name without proper *kavanah* would be better off if he had not been created.[35]

We are not required to familiarize ourselves with the Kabbalistic interpretations of Hashem's name. We must focus on the basic concepts of Hashem's mastery over all. The *Mekubalim* advised contemplating the name of G–d, *Havaya*, while praying. This inspires man's heart with fear of Hashem and purifies his soul.[36]

When speaking of Hashem, we should avoid any resemblance to those of whom it is said, "With his mouth and lips he honors Me, but his heart is distant from Me." *(Yeshaya 29,13)*[37] Our limbs should tremble as we focus on Hashem, Who always was, is and will be.[38]

The Divrei Yechezkel's teeth would chatter every time he said the word "awesome" during prayer. R' Tuvia of Krolli commented that R' Yechezkel was a "Magen Avraham Jew." The Magen Avraham writes that when we say Hashem's name, our whole body should tremble, just as R' Yechezkel visibly trembled each time he said Hashem's name. (Rabbeinu HaKadosh MiShinova)

When someone said the name of Hashem in the presence of R' Chaim Brisker, he would visibly tremble. (Uvdos VeHanhagos LeBais Brisk) His student, R' Baruch Ber Leibowitz, would sometimes faint when he said the name of Hashem. (Mashal HaAvos)

Visualizing the Words and the Concepts

The Men of the Great Assembly who composed the text of the

Shemoneh Esrei numbered one hundred and twenty scholars.

Guided by a spirit of Divine holiness, they invested each word of the liturgy with the power to influence all of creation, from the smallest atomic particle to the most enormous galactic mass. Even more astounding: the impact of the evening *tefillah* is not the same as the impact of the morning prayer, though they may consist of the very same words.

As we pronounce each word, we should picture in our mind's eye a mental image of the shape and form of the actual word. Then we should concentrate on raising the words heavenward to their celestial source, visualizing the words as they stream upward. A person praying in this fashion will make an impact with every word.[39] The *Gemara* refers to the words of prayers as "matters which stand at the pinnacle of the universe," because every phrase of prayer actually rises up to heaven in its shape of letters and words, impacting the entire universe.[40]

Associating pictures with words and sentences is a good way to keep our minds focused on what we are saying. If our minds are full of images associated with what our mouths are saying, our thoughts are less likely to wander.

When you say the blessing *Yotzer HaMeoros*, Who fashions the luminaries, visualize the glory of the heavens – and then consider that they are nothing compared to the might and power of Hashem. When you say the *berachos* for any food or drink you enjoy, enhance your pleasure by imagining what it would be like if the food or drink was not available. Such visualization will create a sense of indebtedness, which, in turn, will flood one's senses with gratitude to Hashem.When a person says the *beracha Shehecheyanu*, Who has kept us alive and preserved us to reach this time, he should imagine himself facing imminent death – thus deepening his appreciation of being alive on such a joyous occasion.

When he says the blessings in the *Amidah* asking Hashem to re-establish the service in the *Bais HaMikdash*, he should imagine the Jewish people bowing to the Divine Presence in the Temple.[41] In the fifth blessing of *Shemoneh Esrei* he should feel compassion for those who do not see the truth, and envision them doing *teshuvah.* He should visualize the ingathering of the Jews, and envision the scholars sitting in their judicial chambers.[42]

During *Shema*, visualize the ultimate in self-sacrifice; visualize walking out on everything you possess in order to live as a Jew. See yourself passing on our traditions to our children, while on the road or at home, when going to sleep or upon awakening. Visualize the binding of *tefillin* on the hand, the centering of the *tefillin* on the forehead and the affixing of *mezuzos* on our doors and gates.

"In every single letter of prayer there are worlds and souls and divinity, and these ascend, binding with each other until a word is formed. Ultimately they unite in a true unity with the Divine. If you engage your soul in the process you will experience great joy and pleasure without limit. The goal of praying with *kavanah* is assisting in the unification of these earthly counterparts of Hashem's creative powers." *(Letter of R' Gershon Kitover)*

R' Moshe Aharon Stern, the Mashgiach of Kaminetz yeshiva, would cry profusely during the prayers on Rosh Hashanah and Yom Kippur, when he said, "One cow... One ram..." One of his students asked him what there was to cry about. The Mashgiach replied, "How is it possible not to cry? I recall the wondrous description of the sacrifices as described in the Talmud, when the Temple existed and we served our most exalted G-d, how is it possible not to cry?" (HaMashgiach MiKaminetz)

The Maggid Mishnah advised R' Yosef Caro to be very careful not to think about anything during prayer, except for the mental image of the words of prayer.

Focus on Hashem

When a plane takes off on a cloudy day, its journey begins on the ground; but it soon rises above the clouds and finds itself in sunshine.[43] When a person begins to pray, he is often surrounded by noise, people, cars, etc. There are thoughts of troubles, business matters, quarrels, competition, desires and hobbies. Once he begins praying, however, there should be only stillness, as if the world around is suddenly silent.[44]

When man is about to begin his prayer, he is alone and frightened, weak and torn by worries that threaten to overwhelm him. When the moment of prayer arrives, he should visualize himself rising to the heavens.[45] He turns to his loving Father in Heaven and admits his frailty, allowing the weighty burdens to slip off his shoulders in the realization that he is not alone.[46]

The supplicant should vividly picture Hashem opposite him, listening to his prayers and taking heed of his heart's meditations. This is a most exalted aspect of prayer.[47] A person who prays with the conscious knowledge that Hashem is with him and cares for him will have his prayers answered. He calls out to Hashem with the confidence of a man calling to his friend, knowing that his friend is always available to help him.

Hashem's glory and greatness is vested in the words of prayer. It is revealed to each of us in accordance with our intellect, if we make the effort. Prayer is a time when Hashem makes Himself known and available to those who seek and long for Him.[48]

When praying, we should be "as if standing before the King." *(Berachos 33)* In some respects, the Kingdom of Heaven can be compared to a kingdom on earth. We are empowered to focus our imagination on this and other images to electrify our emotions. Historically, great, righteous people have used this technique to heighten their prayer experience.[49]

Before beginning our prayers we should visualize ourselves walking towards Yerushalayim, ascending the steps of Temple Mount, entering the *Bais HaMikdash*, moving towards the *Kodesh*

HaKadashim (Holy of Holies), and standing opposite the great and awesome King. Then we should pray to the best of our ability.[50] We should return to that image when necessary, even in the middle of *tefillah*.[51]

We can try visualizing Hashem listening to us like a friend. Just as we can speak to a friend with a few hand movements, by simply lifting the receiver and dialing, so can we speak to Hashem by merely opening the *siddur* and finding the page. Knowing this with certainty endows our prayers with clarity and purity.[52]

Try to imagine the spiritual realm, the various types of angels, the souls of the patriarchs, the prophets, and the righteous of the different generations, and in the center – Hashem's throne. You may be standing in the physical world, but your words are about to embark on a journey into the world of the spiritual. Visualize the impact of your prayers, for when a person prays the joy in heaven is intense.[53]

When we start a blessing and we use the word "*atah*" to address Hashem, we should visualize Him receiving our prayers together with those of the entire Jewish people. Although we may be considered a "ragged child" in comparison to others, nevertheless, we have joined the choir of the angels above in singing the praises of Hashem. Our joy should be so great and our spirit so uplifted that our hearts melt into tears.

A king customarily conceals his majesty in the innermost chambers, with many guards at the doors, so people have to wait for years to see his might and glory. When the king wishes to be revealed to everyone, however, he proclaims throughout his kingdom that they should assemble and stand before him, in order to be shown his majestic glory and the splendor of his greatness.

If anyone were to stand before the king without bothering to look at him, choosing instead to examine his fingernails, how inferior and foolish he would be in everyone's eyes. It dishonors the king if one indicates that his own preoccupations are more important than the pleasure and delight of beholding the king's splendor and glory.

Practical Advice for Saying Berachos with Kavanah

Before beginning and ending a blessing, we should stop to collect our thoughts.[54] At the beginning a blessing, think about its contents and what you want to request from Hashem. Before ending, mentally formulate a final request for the blessing.

For instance, before the first of the *Amidah* blessings you should think about praising Hashem, Who is our G–d and the G–d of our Fathers, Who created everything, Who protected Avraham. Before the second *beracha*, you should think of praising Hashem for the revival of the dead. Before the blessing for wisdom, stop and think for a moment, "Now I am going to ask Hashem for knowledge." Before the blessing for health you should think, "Now I am going to ask Hashem for a full recovery."

In his later years the Chofetz Chaim would pray quite audibly because his hearing was impaired. He could be heard pausing before every blessing in Shemoneh Esrei, in fulfillment of the above recommendation of the Yesod VeShoresh HaAvodah.

It is recommended that we contemplate the connections between the *berachos*.[55] For example: why does the blessing of holiness follow the blessing of the revival of the dead? Holiness enables a person to achieve prophecy. Prophecy enables a person to revive the dead. First one does *teshuvah*; then one asks for forgiveness. Before asking for healing of the body, one seeks a cure for the ills of the spirit.

Rabbi Y.Z. Segal advises that when praying *Shemoneh Esrei,* one should make an effort to focus on the opening blessing. From there one can gradually progress through the remainder of the *prayer*. He also recommends that a person make a concerted effort to increase *kavanah* at selected times. The ideal time for this is Shabbos, for the sanctity inherent in that day makes it a most opportune time for spiritual growth.

In a letter to his son, the *Rambam* mentions the importance of reciting the opening blessing of *Birchas HaMazon* with proper *kavanah*. Surely, the *Rambam's* intent was that his son should initially strive to recite the opening blessing with proper *kavanah*, and then proceed to master the remaining *berachos*.[56]

R' Moshe Shushan would don his turban for every beracha. He would tell his children that they should always wear a hat when they said a beracha for, after all, they were talking to Hashem.

It was his custom to stand near the mezuzah in the aura of its holiness and say his beracha slowly, with great concentration. He told his son that the beracha flows better near the mezuzah. His beracha was so loud that it could be heard out on the street. From the next room, it was possible to hear him crying as he bentched. (Ish Yehudi Haya)

A well-known Mashgiach came upon the Steipler as he was saying the blessing Asher Yatzar. He later commented that the Asher Yatzar he overheard was more intense then his own Shemoneh Esrei prayers. Who knows how many people were healed in the merit of these blessings? (Toldos Yaakov)

R' Eliyahu Lapian would recommend a self-imposed fine for each beracha without *kavanah*.[57]

We should say each *beracha* with eagerness and joy, simply because we have the privilege of praising Hashem.[58] We should be very specific about our requests.[59] At the same time, however, a person should be careful not to concentrate only on blessings of request, while neglecting the blessings of praise. A person who does so will find that accusing angels will block his prayers.[60]

Other Useful Strategies

Here are some additional strategies for ensuring that our prayers succeed.

• Praying with a pleasing melody gives each phrase a life of its own. Use an earnest melody for requests and a joyous melody for praise. Let your tunes express your yearning for the Master of the

Universe.[61]

R' Raphael Baruch Toledano of Meknes would rise in the middle of the night for Tikun Chatzos, the midnight prayers of mourning. While groveling in the ashes, he would wail bitterly for the destruction of the Bais HaMikdash and the exile of the Shechinah. After rising from the ground, he would sing many heartfelt melodies of his own composition, which reflected the longings of his soul. (Oros MiMizrach)

• One way of remaining focused is to invest each blessing of *Shemoneh Esrei* with personal details. We should specify our indebtedness, embellish our praise, and detail our requests. This will help us keep our minds on the prayer we are saying.[62]

R' Shmuel Shenker wanted R' Simcha Zisel of Kelm to advise him whether he should move to Eretz Yisrael or not. R' Simcha Zisel told him to return after the evening prayer for his reply. During Maariv, he would focus on the words of the prayer, "Endow us with good advice," requesting the ability to counsel R' Shmuel judiciously. (Siach Yisrael, page 341)

• One should contemplate an extraordinary aspect of nature.[63] In our generation, new scientific and technological wonders of the Creator are revealed to us regularly and can be used as a focal point of our appreciative meditations.[64] Consider how Hashem's glory fills the whole universe, and how we ourselves exist within Him and His holiness. The more often we reflect on this, the easier it will be to stimulate our souls to speak to Hashem.[65]

• If a person is concerned that he may not have *davened* with the proper *kavanah*, he should pay careful attention to the repetition of the *chazan*, at which time it is less likely that negative forces will distract him.[66]

[1] Or Yechezkel Emunah, page 309

[2] Orchos Chaim, Laws of Tefillah

[3] Peleh Yoetz

[4] Alei Shor, Book I

[5] Shaloh HaKadosh Tamid, Ner Mitzvah

[6] Bava Basra 154

[7] El Hamekoros, Volume 2, page 115

[8] Rabbi Lopes Cardozo, *Between Silence and Speech*, Chapter 11

[9] Yesod VeShoresh HaAvodah

[10] Olas Tamid

[11] Bais Tefillah

[12] Charedim 6, 79

[13] Shaloh Ha'Kadosh, Tamid, Ner Mitzvah

[14] Shemos Rabah 22

[15] Yevamos 105, 2

[16] Berachos 30

[17] Hilchos Tefilah, 4

[18] Nefesh Ha'Chayim Shaar 2, chapter 12

[19] Tzavaas HaRivash

[20] Bais Elokim 83

[21] Shalmei Tzibbur, Hilchos Tefillah and Kavanah

[22] Alei Shur Part I

[23] Yesod VeShoresh HaAvodah, Chapter 3

[24] Me'Am Loez

[25] Ben Ish Chai, Halachos

[26] Kaf HaChaim 98,1,2

[27] Nesivos Emunah II, page 82

[28] Samak 11

[29] Marbitzei Torah U'Mussar

[30] Shaarei Teshuvah 1,8

[31] Kol Bo 11; Yesod VeShoresh HaAvodah 2,2; Mishnas R' Aharon, Part II, page 80

[32] Rabenu Yona, Igeres HaTeshuvah

[33] Inyonei Tefillah, Tochachas Mussar

[34] Siddur Ari, R' Yehoshua Zev Segal on Shaarei Teshuvah

[35] Zohar, Yisro

[36] Shevet Mussar, chapter 31

[37] Orchos Chaim 38

[38] Rokeach, Yesod VeShoresh HaAvodah

[39] Nefesh HaChaim 2,11

[40] Nefesh HaChaim 2,13

[41] Kuzari 3

[42] Hearas HaTefillah

[43] HeAras Tefillah

[44] Pathways, Rabbi S. Wolbe, page 63

[45] Rabenu Yona, Berachos

[46] HeAras Tefillah

[47] Shaloh HaKadosh; Igros Volume I, 23

[48] Igeres HaKodesh, chapter 24

[49] Adapted from Chovas HaTalmidim

[50] Bais Tefillah

[51] Orach Chaim 95,2; Yesod VeShoresh HaAvodah 5,1

[52] Adapted from Meiri on Berachos 30

[53] Tur Orach Chaim 125

[54] Yesod VeShoresh HaAvodah, chapter 5

[55] R' Naftali Amsterdam based on Megilah 17

[56] Yirah VeDaas, Tu BeShevat

[57] Birkas Avraham

[58] Shem Olam

[59] Bais Tefillah

[60] Sefer HaChassidim 158; Mabit; Derech Hashem 1,82

[61] Sefer Chassidim, chapter 158; Bais Tefillah; Sefer HaIkarim, Maamar 4, 23

[62] Hearas HaTefillah

[63] Avodas HaTefillah, in the name of R' Moshe Feinstein, page 71

[64] Heard from Rabbi Avigdor Miller

[65] Chovos HaTalmidim, chapter 9

[66] Shearim BeTefillah

Knowing What to Ask

The Content of Prayer

During the course of every day, both spontaneously and at regular intervals, a person should approach Hashem without hesitation, speaking to Him in his own words. He should say a short *tefilah* and "Cast our burden on Hashem." *(Tehillim 55:23)*

One Rosh Chodesh Elul, Baba Sali asked to be taken to the Kotel immediately. "My soul yearns to be at the Kotel. I must get there quickly before it is too late."

During the ride from Netivot to Yerushalayim, the Rav was nervous and impatient. When they finally arrived in Yerushalayim, the Rav got out of the car immediately and sat down to rest on a chair that had been brought over for him. He bent his head forward, leaning on his hands. After several silent moments, he was ready to return, without even going up to the Kotel itself.

"I have completed my tefilah," he said. "Now it is time to go home."

On the way home he was calm and relaxed. The others could not comprehend his joy and serenity. All the Rav said was, "I have prayed." At home he added, "Baruch Hashem, everything will be all right now." (Baba Sali)

The Power of Prayer

Prayer saves people's lives. When the Jewish people sinned with the golden calf, Hashem wanted to destroy them, but Moshe's prayers saved them.[1] Yaakov battled *Shechem* side by side with his sons, but his weapons were words of prayer.[2]

Prayer enables barren women to give birth, as we see from Rivka[3] and Chana.[4] The Torah tells us that Yitzchak and Rivka prayed because Rivka was barren.[5] Why doesn't the verse describe the situation the other way around – Rivka was barren, and therefore they prayed? *Rabenu* Bachya explains that Hashem wanted to hear their prayers, so He did not grant Rivka children.

Prayer halts famine, resulting from the sin of counting the Jewish people, as we learn from David.[6] Chizkiyah utilized the power of prayer once to overpower *Sancheriv* and his mighty army[7] and again to cure himself when he was sick.[8]

A gentile boat out at sea had one Jewish child aboard. A great storm arose, and everyone took their idols in their hands and cried out to them-to no avail. Realizing the futility of their attempts, the idolaters said to the Jew, "Get up and call to your G-d, for we have heard that He answers you when you cry out to Him, and that He is strong." The child began to pray with all his heart. Hashem accepted his prayers, and the sea quieted. (Yerushalmi Berachos, Chapter 9, Halacha 1)

A man with a sick daughter came to R' Shlomo Zalmen Auerbach to ask him to pray for his daughter, for the doctors despaired of her life. R' Shlomo Zalmen encouraged him, blessed her and wished them both well. After they left, he took a Tehillim and poured out his heart on behalf of the sick child.

The next morning, the man returned with good news. The girl had improved dramatically, and the doctors were optimistic. He was convinced that it was a miracle.

Rabbi Shlomo Zalmen quoted the Gemara which says that one should ask a wise person to daven on behalf of someone who is ill. (Bava Basra 116) R' Shlomo Zalmen asked, "Why is he not told to go to a tzaddik, a righteous person?"

Rabbi Eliyahu Kletzk of Lublin explains that if he went to a tzaddik to receive a blessing and the patient recovered, the tzaddik would be convinced that he was a miracle worker. But when a wise person's prayers are fulfilled, he attributes it to the power of prayer. (HaMaor HaGadol)

A Total Salvation

We should continue to *daven* until Hashem has sent us a complete salvation. Many people are satisfied with partial reprieves. But why ask that the surgery should be successful, if we can request that the surgery not be required at all? Why ask for a passable *shidduch* when we can request the very best?

While the Czar was reviewing the troops, an enemy soldier took aim at him. A brave Russian soldier threw himself at the Czar, knocked him down, and saved his life. The grateful Czar told the soldier that he would grant any request.

The soldier complained that the sergeant was very cruel to him and asked the Czar to order the sergeant to treat him more kindly. He begged to receive his daily meals, which he required for his sustenance.

"Fool!" laughed his companions. "You should have asked to be made an officer. Then you would have been responsible only to the Czar, and the sergeant would have had to take orders from you! And as for your meals-all soldiers are sustained by the Czar!"

Throughout the centuries, great *tzaddikim* were not satisfied with halfway measures. They waited for Hashem to extricate them totally from their difficulties, like *Choni Ha' Me'agel*[9] who refused to leave the circle until Hashem sent the right type of rain, neither too heavy nor too light.[10]

The elders of Egypt recorded the story of Judge Kadi Al-Akshir, who was sent from Constantinople. He hated the Jews with all his heart and soul and caused them so much distress that they could not bear it any longer.

In response to his brethren's plight, the great tzaddik R' Moshe Aldamuhi went to prostrate himself at the tombs of the holy forefathers in that land. With hoes and spades, he and his attendant dug a large hole in the middle of the graveyard and descended into it.

There, in the pit, R' Moshe prayed, "I command you, the dead, by the name of the Lord, G–d of the living and the dead, that you should pray with me as we pray for you three times a day, saying: 'Blessed are You, O Lord, who brings the dead to life!' So pray with me on behalf of the Jews who are being oppressed in such a terrible fashion." And he prayed there until the tombstones in the graveyard rocked in their places.

When R' Moshe ended his prayer, he said to his attendant, "Go to the city and see if there have been any new developments today. I shall wait here." When the attendant reached Alqarpa, where the Moslem notables are buried, he saw a huge crowd. A Moslem said to him, "Turn back, Jew, for you cannot pass here."

"What is all the commotion about?" the attendant asked.

"Surely you must have heard – the Kadi Al-Ashkir died suddenly! Now the elders of his household and all the elders of Egypt have come to bury him here." At this, the attendant clapped his hands together in wonder and wept, while his heart rejoiced. He hurried back to the graveyard to tell the rabbi the good news. (Min Hamekoros)

A shochet living in Yerushalayim was having a very hard

time making ends meet. R' Yosef Chaim Sonnenfeld advised him to say the section dealing with the falling of 'man' after his prayers. A few weeks later, the man returned. He had followed the Rav's instructions, but he had only received a job offer in the new city of Tel Aviv, which he had to refuse for lack of a proper environment to educate charedi children.

R' Yosef Chaim praised the man for his resolve and added, "Keep praying for something more suitable." A few days later the shochet received a respectable position in Yerushalayim, which he retained for the rest of his life. (HaIsh Al HaChomos)

Pray to Serve Hashem Better

Prayer is called "service of the heart" because the desire of our heart defines the prayer that comes from our lips. What is true prayer? When we truly desire to serve Hashem, and our entreaties are solely to facilitate this goal.[11]

A foreman wishing for more comfortable working conditions knows that approaching his superior directly will prove unsuccessful. Instead, he points out to the manager that in the summer, productivity declines. He suggests that air-conditioning be installed so output will improve.

We are adjured to keep our eyes lowered and our heart upraised.[12] The *Chida* explains that when a person makes material requests, his focus should be above and beyond his physical sphere. In other words, we request health, sustenance and life only as a means of serving Hashem.[13]

"I believe in You!" we should say during *davening*. "I am here to do Your will! I am here to offer all that I am and all that I can accomplish. But I lack the resources to fulfill the mitzvos I must keep. If I were to receive help, I would be able to fulfill more of Your will and serve You better. With this help, I will study Your Torah and help Your people. Please give me money so I can support the causes that You want accomplished, and I will have no need to flatter others."[14]

If one davens sincerely for something that brings honor to Hashem, such as the ability to study Torah, then Hashem will listen – even if he has no merit.[15] Our prayers should not be sullied by ulterior motives; the sole intent should be that Hashem strengthen us so we may better serve Him.[16]

In his commentary on the blessing Chonen HaDaas, the Rebbe Reb Yonasan movingly says: A person should shed streams of tears, requesting that Hashem grant him understanding as an unearned gift. When a scholar requests understanding with a heart open to the truth of Torah, and not, G–d forbid, to be used to advance his own agenda at the expense of others, Hashem will grant his request.

Can one ask for wisdom and then use it in ways that are not pleasing to Hashem, by flaunting his wisdom and enjoying the humiliation of others? This is like buying a hammer and millstone with money borrowed from a friend, then making a tremendous racket so the same friend cannot sleep all night.

Pray for Hashem's Kingship

The prayers of *Rosh Hashanah* are organized around the theme of restoring Hashem's kingship as it was prior to the sin of Adam.[17] R' Chaim Volozhiner explains this concept using a parable.

A king ruled over a country whose main industry was construction materials. All builders would buy supplies at the palace. The king was a good-hearted ruler who was very generous with the people of his land. He had a minister who was very knowledgeable in the field of construction. He had been educated in the palace and raised to Master Builder by the king himself.

The minister once approached the king with a suggestion. He felt so indebted to the king that he had come up with a plan to somehow repay the king for his generosity. He wished to build the king a palace in his honor. The king was overjoyed, and allowed the minister to help himself to supplies from the king's reserves.

Every day the minister was seen helping himself to various supplies. Of course he paid nothing. The other buyers wondered why he was given anything he wanted without anyone even recording the transactions, while they had to pay up front in cash. When they found out that he was building a palace for the king, they finally understood why he had free access to the supplies.

On *Rosh Hashanah* we approach Hashem, offering to build Him a habitation in this world where He can reign as king. When we do this in earnest appreciation of His greatness, Hashem is pleased with us. He then readily opens His storehouse, granting children, life and sustenance so we can readily create the kingdom below.

"I am for my beloved, and my beloved is for me." When my aim is to please my beloved, then my beloved supplies me with unlimited blessing and success.[18]

The *Rosh Hashanah* prayers are the benchmark for prayers said throughout the year. Rabbi Naftali of Ropshitz points out that even as we come before Hashem with a variety of petty requests, the essence of our prayers should be "That all may honor His Glorious Name…That all accept the yoke of His Kingdom…That He will reign over us all speedily forever and ever…" All our other requests will then be fulfilled automatically.

With the commitment to fashion Hashem's kingdom, our prayers have the strength to bring abundant material blessing to the world for the entire year; without this commitment, our prayers are feeble.[19]

Praying for the Divine's Anguish

When the Jewish people suffer, the *Shechinah* suffers along with them.[20] In *Shir HaShirim*, the Jewish people are referred to as Hashem's twin.[21] When one twin suffers the other one feels pain as well. When we *daven* to relieve our own suffering, we must also pray that the *Shechinah* return to her place and the honor of Hashem be revealed in this world.[22]

Any person whose prayer is charged by the anguish the *Shechinah* feels has his prayers answered.[23] If the Jewish people would feel such sympathy to the point of being oblivious to their own privations, we would be redeemed immediately. Since we pray for all sorts of trivial things instead, we achieve only a partial salvation.[24]

The *Midrash* on the verse in *Tehillim*, "My heart rejoices in your salvation," *(Tehillim 13:6)* points out that the salvation of Hashem is the salvation of the Jewish people.[25] Our prayer should be an attempt to bring blessing and light to the universe and to eradicate the spirit of impurity, resulting in salvation for all. We should think of our souls as a part of the Divine presence, like a drop in the sea; then pray for the needs of the greater whole, for the Divine presence.[26]

Davening on Behalf of Others

Each day a person should pray on behalf of the sick to recover, and on behalf of the well that they not fall sick. He should pray that Hashem save the Jewish people from the gentiles, from poverty and from any calamity. He should pray for those imprisoned, for women in the throes of childbirth, for the Jews lost amongst the gentiles. For those who are childless he should request children; for those who have children he should pray that the children live a G–d fearing life. He should request that

Hashem protect the Jewish people, and avenge the wrongs committed against us, and that He should receive our repentance.[27] We should pray for peace, that there be no conflict among Jews, no jealousy, no hate and no competition. We should all be beloved to each other, so all Jews are united as one.[28]

Each Erev Rosh Chodesh, R' Yehuda Tzedaka organized a Yom Kippur Katan prayer group in the yeshiva, where the students would pray for the welfare of the Jewish people. They would say the traditional prayers, followed by the entire sefer Tehillim. The pious, ascetic R' Avraham Harari Raful would lead the prayers. R' Yehuda would try to arouse the gathering to repentance with words of mussar. He would then send his students back to the study hall, saying, "The best way to ensure that our prayers will have an impact is to follow them with enthusiastic study."

When he realized that some of the young men were not attending the prayer session perhaps because they felt that it unnecessarily disturbed their studies. R' Yehuda spoke with them privately. He explained that his own teacher, Rabbeinu Ezra Ettia, had instituted this custom, based on a long standing practice in the city of Yerushalayim, to pray for compassion and peace on the behalf all Jews on that day. (Kaf HaChaim in the name of the Pri Chodosh 417,13; VeZos LeYehuda)

If we do not take our *siddur* or *Tehillim* in hand to pray on behalf of others, it indicates that either we do not believe in the power of prayer — or that we are indifferent to the pain of our friend, G–d forbid. When we daven for the greater benefit of our fellow Jews, we ourselves benefit. The *Maggid* of Dubno explained this with a parable: If a fire erupted in a city and everyone rushed to extinguish the fire, the city would be saved. But if each individual were to rush to his own house, the fire would get bigger and bigger, eventually ravaging the city. If we all pray for the general welfare of the community, then all are saved. If we pray only for ourselves, then no one is saved.[29]

> *When R' Yaakov Yisrael Kanievsky was ill, he was visited by a man who was also seriously ill. The Steipler asked for water to wash his hands. He then said to the sick man, "Let us say some Tehillim together for your recovery and mine." They said "Shir hamaalos beshuv Hashem es shivas Tziyon" and "Mizmor shir chanukas habayis leDovid," chapters 126 and 30. Then R' Yaakov Yisrael gave the man a warm beracha, and the visitor left. (Toldos Yaakov)*

Whoever is able to arouse Hashem's compassion for a friend and does not do so is called a sinner.[30] Any *tefilah* that does not include supplications for others is not a *tefilah*.[31] When a person does not feel the pain of others, it is not fitting that his *tefilah* be answered. He should think, "If I were the one suffering, G–d forbid, I would daven for relief."[32] Sensitivity to others should be cultivated. When passing a handicapped or needy person on the street, one should say a short prayer on his behalf.

Praiseworthy is the one who *davens* for his neighbor when he needs the same thing. When Avraham *davened* for Avimelech, his own wife Sarah bore a child.[33] When Iyov *davened* for his friend, Hashem improved his own fortunes.[34]

When a person *davens* for himself, he is motivated by selfish thoughts. But when he turns to Hashem on behalf of his friend, he is not furthering his own agenda. Hashem first responds to his selflessness, then turns His attention to those for whom he *davens*.[35]

It is best to pray in the plural. By praying for the greater good of all of *bnei Yisrael*, we can fully achieve Hashem's purpose in creating the world.[36] When Israel's condition deteriorates, Hashem's name is desecrated. When His nation is secure, He is blessed, because all humanity recognizes that success lies in the service of Hashem.

Strict judgment is generally reserved for the individual, so it is best to join in prayer with others. Within a large group there will always be people who arouse Hashem's compassion, which then spills over to the others. The woman of Shunamis said to Elisha, "In the midst of my people I sit." To avoid strict justice, she linked her prayers to those of her contemporaries and benefited from Hashem's indulgence.[37]

When Avraham interceded for the people of Sodom, he took the risk of angering Hashem with his continued entreaties, as he repeated, "Please don't get angry." *(Beraishis 18:32)*[38] Avraham taught us the importance of praying for others, while at the same time genetically imprinting this type of selflessness on the Jewish people.[39]

After asking for a king, the Jewish people asked Shmuel to pray on their behalf. Despite the fact that they had disgraced Shmuel and sinned against Hashem, Shmuel continued to pray for them. He prayed for the Jews even though they had hurt him, serving as an example to the nation to pray even on behalf of those who harmed them.[40]

In days of yore, if a person killed a man accidentally, he was required to flee to a city of refuge where he remained until the death of the *Kohen Gadol*.[41] The mother of the *Kohen Gadol* would bring food and clothing to these exiles so they would not pray that her son should die.

The *Kohen Gadol* should beseech Hashem from the outset that no such accidents occur during his lifetime.[42] If the *Kohen* was derelict in his duty and he failed to daven, accidental deaths occurred. It is fitting, therefore, that those who accidentally killed someone would pray that the *Kohen Gadol* should die an early death, to be replaced with a more sensitive *Kohen*. It was hoped that the new *Kohen Gadol* would beseech Hashem to spare the Jews accidental deaths and a lifetime in exile. Pleas of those who accidently killed someone, against a High Priest who prayed as he should have were ignored.

The great Torah scholars of our generation have assumed the *Kohen's* role. The *Rambam*, in the laws of *shemitah* and *yovel*, rules that those who study Torah are like the *Levi'im* and *Kohanim* of their generation. When a person has a sick relative in his home, he is told to go to a scholar and ask him to turn to G–d for compassion on behalf of the patient.[43] "The anger of the King [induces] the angel of death, a wise man atones." *(Mishlei 16,14)* The wise man, or the *Kohen Gadol*, is obligated to pray for his generation when the angel of death is ready to strike. If the leader of the generation does not fulfill his obligation to evoke compassion for others, Hashem will find someone else to replace him.[44]

When a man was devoured by a lion three hundred *parsas* (12-14 miles) from R' Yehoshua ben Levi, *Eliyahu HaNavi* did not speak to R' Yehoshua for three days. The accident was his responsibility, since his prayers had the power to protect his fellow Jews within a circumference of three hundred *parsas*. *Eliyahu HaNavi* punished him by excommunicating him for three days.[45]

On his first visit to Radin, Rav Kahaneman became a devoted disciple of the Chofetz Chaim. During his first glimpse of the great tzaddik, he saw the Chofetz Chaim standing in the corner, tears flowing to the ground, as he wept on behalf of a woman having difficulty giving birth. He was so impressed by the Chofetz Chaim's profound dedication to his fellow Jew that he immediately resolved to take him as his mentor and guide. (As told by his student Rabbi Yashar)

Praying for Someone to Do *Teshuvah*

When confessing our wrongdoings, we use the plural form: "We have sinned." When one Jew sins, it is as if everyone sinned.[46]

Since all our souls are interconnected, we can also *daven* for someone else to do *teshuvah*. The proper place to insert this request is in the blessing *Hashivenu Avinu* in the *Amidah* prayer. We are obligated to do all in our power to prevent our fellow Jews from being sentenced to *Gehinnom*.

Abba Chilkiya was the righteous grandson of Choni Hamagol. When Abba Chilkiya and his wife prayed for rain on behalf of the Jewish people, the prayers of Abba Chilkiya's wife were answered first. The Gemara explains that because women are at home, they have more opportunities to give charity. They are more likely to give a pauper food, instead of money, so he can immediately benefit. (Taanis 23a) R' Elazar Ashkenazi explains that her prayers were answered first because she prayed that the wicked in her neighborhood should repent. (Charedim Chapter 68)

Reb Moshe Alshich had a son who converted to Christianity. The Ari taught the bereaved father a tefillah that would arouse his son to do teshuvah. He eventually returned to his people. (Shaar Ruach Ha'Kodesh page 76)

Rabbi Raphael Baruch Toledano, Rav in Meknes, would set aside time to pray for the coming of Mashiach and for the spiritual and material success of the Jewish people. He also *would beseech Hashem with copious tears to inspire sinners to do teshuvah. (Oros MiMizrach)*

Each soul includes a portion of all other Jewish souls. Praying for others to do *teshuvah* is like praying for part of your own soul to repent. Acting in a way that is spiritually conducive to *teshuvah* can also bring your neighbor to *teshuvah*.[48]

A young secular Jew once entered the shul of R' Aharon Roth, searching for a business associate. The Rebbe was davening Hallel. As usual, he davened with great excitement, and his melodious exaltations filled the shul.

The words pierced the soul of the visitor and stirred his very essence. He was so deeply affected by the Rebbe's moving Hallel that he resolved to repent. After the Rebbe had finished his prayers, the young man approached him for recommendations on how to adopt a religious lifestyle. R' Aharon advised him to break off with his secular friends and abandon his evil deeds. He asked that the man pledge to join their prayers daily. After a short time, the young man became fully committed to Judaism. (Siach Yisrael quoting Toldos Aharon)

Every devout Jew should be motivated by a concern for the good of the entire generation, and imbued with a desire to benefit and protect it. Hashem does not desire the destruction of the wicked; the pious are obligated to pray for their atonement.

In the midst of the tragic struggle to prevent the spiritual annihilation of the Jews of Teiman and Morocco by the Israeli government, R' Reuven Grozovsky discovered that Ben Gurion would be visiting the United States. He was determined to make a statement regarding the cruelty with which these young children were being forced to abandon their religion. He organized a delegation of Rabbis and community activists to visit the Prime Minister and express their objection to the government policy.

Among the proposed delegates were some who hoped to gain honor and prestige from this visit. R' Reuven was concerned that this might prevent them from speaking bluntly about the heinous crime.

The night before the meeting, after fasting all day, he visited each member of the delegation personally. R' Reuven wanted to inspire them with the magnitude of their mission and the import of its consequences. He talked and talked all through the night, until each one understood the gravity of the matter.

Sunrise found him praying from a book of Tehillim with heart-rending tears. He then visited one last influential member of the delegation. Finally he hurried to Yeshiva Torah Vodaas and told the boys to say Tehillim for the success of the mission. He fasted again on that day until after the meeting with Ben Gurion. All this occurred against a background of great personal crisis for him and his family. (*Marbitzei Torah U'Mussar*)

The more we love our fellow Jews, the more Hashem loves us. Hashem applauds those who pray that harsh decrees be revoked and that the gates of blessing be opened. It is like a father who loves no one more than the man who has a genuine love for his sons.[49]

R' Yosef Chaim Sonnenfeld would not react to a sinner with scorn, but with the compassion one might have for a handicapped individual. While he hated the wicked deeds of those who turned their backs on religion, he never exhibited any negativity toward them.[50] R' Yosef Chaim was always going out of his way to assist even those individuals who were so brazen as to slander him and sought to destroy everything he held dear. He unrestrainedly loved every Jew.

R' Yosef Chaim was leaving Shaarei Tzedek Hospital one Tu BeShevat when he and R' Moshe Blau noticed a large group of secular school children marching toward them, singing Hebrew songs.

Knowing that the sight of several thousand irreligious children would cause R' Chaim anguish, R' Moshe asked if the Rav would like to return to the building. "No," he replied. "They are Jewish children, aren't they?"

As the children were marching four abreast on the narrow road, all the pedestrians had to wait until they passed. Meanwhile, R' Chaim's mouth was moving steadily. R' Moshe leaned forward so he could hear his words. He was saying, "May Hashem add upon you, upon you and upon your children! May you be blessed by Hashem, Maker of heaven and earth." (Tehillim 115,14-15) He repeated these blessings over and over again, until the last child in the long procession had passed. (Od Yosef Chai)

Prayers for a sinner who is no longer among the living are very effective – his soul is ejected from *Gehinnom* like an arrow from a bow.[51] One is forbidden to pray that a wicked Jew die, as Beruriah reminded her husband when wicked neighbors made their lives difficult. Rather, we should pray that the wicked repent for their evil deeds.[52]

We may also pray for a gentile, because even he can make a major contribution to the Jewish world. If Terach, father of Avraham, had not lived, then the Jewish people would never have come into being and the Torah would never have been given.[53] Avraham Avinu himself prayed for the people of Sodom and for Avimelech.

Praying for the Dead

The *Yesod VeShoresh HaAvodah* would say the following prayer regularly: "Master of the world, May it be Your will that You fashion a pure garment for the soul of my father, my teacher, the soul of my mother, my teacher and the soul of my teacher, my Rebbe. May their souls rise higher and higher in Gan Eden. Amen." *(Tzavaah 11)*

We regularly bless the dead and *daven* for them.[54] The *Minchas*

Eluzar rules that one may mention a departed father in the blessing *HaRachaman* in *Birkas HaMazon*. R' Yechezkel Levenstein would recommend that admirers of a departed individual undertake to study on behalf of his or her soul. He felt that a eulogy should include *Tehillim* and an arousal to take action, thus saving the soul of the deceased from harsh judgement.[55] In turn, the dead pray for the living as well.

R' Elchonon Wasserman traveled to Telshe to eulogize his brother-in-law whom he had greatly admired. He arrived before Shabbos. On Shabbos afternoon he gave a lecture to the bochurim. He suddenly removed his watch and said, "Shabbos is now over, R' Shalom is now being led to judgment. Let us all say Tehillim on his behalf!" (Or Elchonon)

About two years before his death, R' Ben Zion Shapira suffered a stroke. When his family saw that his situation was deteriorating, they wanted to add a name. The choleh claimed it wasn't necessary. He had seen R' Zalman, son of R' Nachum, together with R' Yosef Chaim Sonnenfeld davening on his behalf in a dream. "I feel confident that Hashem will now give me a recovery," he said. Indeed, from that day on his situation improved dramatically.

Praying for the Sick

A person should pray on behalf of the sick in his city and for all the sick among the Jewish people. The Jewish people are considered to be one soul and one body; if one person is ill, then a part of all of us is ill.

Different prayers may be said for people of different character. Pray that the virtuous person recover in the merit of his good deeds. Pray that the wicked person recover so he can do *teshuvah*. Pray that Hashem replenish the strength of Torah scholars so they may continue to labor in their studies.[56]

The *mitzvah* of *bikur cholim* exists to encourage us to pray for the *choleh's* speedy recovery.[57] A person who does not visit a sick person is considered to have shed his blood. If he does not view his friend's misery with his own eyes, he will not pray properly on his behalf, and his friend may die. Rabbi Shlomo Zalmen Auerbach would pray for the ill at their bedside, allowing the sight of the patient's suffering to arouse more heartfelt prayers. Similarly, the *Midrash* informs us that a praying battalion would accompany the soldiers to the battlefield.[58] Prayers said at the front would be more heartfelt then those said in the safety of home.[59]

Many souls stand ready to indict those who did not pray for the sick's recovery; whoever does pray fulfills the positive commandment of being compassionate.[60] We do not always instinctively react with pain when we hear that someone is ill. The *Chazon Ish* recommends that we *daven* for others even if we don't really feel their pain, for eventually we will come to sincere prayers on behalf of others.[61] And if the ill person is a scholar, we are even obligated to exhaust ourselves *davening* on his behalf.

R' Akiva Eiger was once asked to daven on behalf of a sick person. The family of the ill person received a letter from R' Akiva asking if he had been given the right name. He had prayed and received no response. He concluded that there must have been an error. Not for one moment did he consider that his prayers might not have been answered. (Igros Sofrim 47 with commentary of R' Shlomo Wolbe)

Rav Yisrael Zev Gustman was davening for someone undergoing a difficult operation. He suddenly rushed to the Aron Kodesh, put his head inside and continued in his recital of Tehillim. Afterward, his students learned that the patient's blood pressure had dropped dangerously low at the exact moment that Rav Gustman had rushed to the Aron. In time, the person recovered completely.

Rabbi Yechezkel Mertz attended the funeral of a man who had died in his prime. Before leaving, he went over to the freshly dug grave and was overheard begging for forgiveness for not having prayed enough on behalf of the deceased.

When R' Yehuda Tzedaka was approached for a blessing by someone who was ill, he took the time to comfort the petitioner. He would offer financial help and was ready to contact a doctor if necessary. After relieving the patient's immediate concerns, he would turn to heartfelt prayer for his recovery.

When R' Akiva Eiger was Rav of Posen, he found it difficult to visit the sick as often as he would have liked. He hired two people to visit the sick daily and minister to their needs. They reported back to him with the name of those who were ill, so he could pray on their behalf. (Chut HaMeshulash)

Praying for Mashiach

Our sages regularly point out the importance of praying for *Mashiach*. All prayers for redemption throughout the generations are gathered together by Hashem. Each prayer and sigh insures our link to the coming of *Mashiach*;[62] they therefore deserve our most intense efforts.[63]

All our different needs and requests will be fulfilled with the coming of *Mashiach*. R' Yechezkel Levenstein would ask others to pray that he merit greeting *Mashiach*.[64]

The Chacham Menachem Moshe, author of Sheves Chaim, was known for his heartfelt prayers for the redemption. His students still gather once a week to daven for the redemption at the Kosel. (Chacham Menachem Menashe)

R' Sulamon Mutzapi would focus on praying for the end of

the exile, an end to the suffering of the Jewish people. During World War II, he spent hours and hours at the Kosel praying for the redemption. (Olamo shel Tzaddik)

When R' Velvel of Brisk would say the blessings on the haftorah, "On His throne no stranger will sit, and others will not inherit His honor," he would cry copious tears. He was so overcome with emotion that he had to wait a few moments until he could continue. (Uvdos VeHanhagos LeBais Brisk)

Adding Personal Requests in our Prayers

Torah knowledge, fear of G–d and good character traits for himself and his children all enter the realm of personal requests. One should pray for a *shidduch*, for financial success, for easing of pain. If one has nothing particular in mind, he should pray that Hashem lead him down the straight and narrow path, and spare him from evil thoughts.[65] If one is celebrating a joyous occasion he should beseech Hashem to insure that the joy be lasting.

The *Yaaros Devash* recommends that a person beg Hashem to help him succeed in all that he plans to do during the course of the day. He should formulate his own prayer in the language he is most comfortable with, a prayer that emanates from the depths of his heart. Various *siddurim* list versions of personal prayers. Praying for everyday success will strengthen our understanding that we are not dependent on random events or on our own efforts. We are utterly dependent on Hashem, as it says, "A person does not bang his finger unless it has been decreed above." *(Chulin 7)*[66]

> *When a child wants something expensive like a silk coat, he asks his father. When he wants something trivial like cake, he again unashamedly asks his father. After all, it is his father. We are children of Hashem and Hashem is our Father. We need not be embarrassed to ask for something trivial, for from whom else can we ask? (Birchas Avraham, Lech Lecha)*

The *Midrash* suggests that we supplicate Hashem for only one thing at a time.[67] The *Zohar* adds that we should be specific in our requests, and not speak in generalities.[68] We learn this from Yaakov, who prayed in specific detail that Hashem save him from his brother, from Esav, whom he greatly feared him.[69]

The *Sefer HaChassidim* and the *Shaloh HaKadosh* recommend that we add a personal request in the vernacular to all our prayers, so we will pay more careful attention to the words we are saying.[70] The injunction in *Avos* not to make our prayers "fixed"[71] requires that we vary them by inserting different personal requests.[72] These requests could also be inserted briefly before the conclusion of each *beracha*.[73]

> *R' Yechezkel Abramsky cried a lot during his prayers. In Shemoneh Esrei he would add his own requests in Yiddish for the preservation of all yeshivos. He would daven for the sick, and for himself, he would beseech Hashem for success in learning. (Knesses Yisrael)*

There are several places throughout *davening* to make extended personal requests. The author of *Chayei Adam* recommends that we insert our personal requests prior to the words "*asei lemaan shimecha*" at the end of the *Amidah* prayer.[74] The blessing *Shema Koleinu* is also an appropriate place.

R' Pinchas of Koretz was once overheard prior to the completion of Shemoneh Esrei asking Hashem that "the maid should return." Among his students were many knowledgeable Kabbalists, but they found nothing in the sources to justify the request as a Kabbalistic formula. Finally they asked the Rebbe what profound petitions were encoded in those words. The Rebbe replied that he had simply put in a request to Hashem that their cleaning lady should come back, as the Rebbetzin did not have the strength to do the cleaning herself.

Asking Hashem to Do as He Sees Fit

To temper our requests for wide spectrums of blessings, we should add a prayer that Hashem confer only good upon us.[75] Our perception is limited – only Hashem knows what is truly good for us. The Jew who is ready to receive everything that Hashem sends his way, with good grace, will merit perceiving the destruction of evil and the splendor of true good.[76]

The *Gemara* gives an example of this type of prayer. "Master of the Universe, do Your will in the Heaven above, delight those that fear you below, and do what is good in Your eyes." *(Berachos 29)*

"Rabbi Yehoshua said, 'Listen to the outcry *(shavas)* of Your people Israel, and quickly respond to their request.' Rabbi Eluzar son of Rabbi Tzadok said, 'Listen to the shout *(tzaakas)* of Your people Israel, and quickly respond to their request.'" *(Berachos 29)* What is the significance of the small change from outcry to shout? The *Ksav VeHaKabala* explains the distinction: Outcry *(shavah)* refers to a specific petition for the resolution of a specific problem, whereas shout *(tzeakah)* is a scream, an expression of pain and an appeal for help — any kind of help. Rabbi Eluzar's wording recommends that a person should simply call out to Hashem, without suggesting how his dilemma should be resolved.[66]

This is the meaning of King David's words, "To Hashem the salvation." *(Tehillim 3,9)* It is inappropriate to advise Hashem how to extricate us from our dilemma. We should simply throw ourselves on His mercy, and let Him decide how to save us from our pressing problems.[78]

In case we make inappropriate requests, we ask Hashem to listen only to the pain of our outcry, and not to the contents.[79] Our sages teach us that we should utter a blessing following unpleasant events just as we do after positive events.[80] Only Hashem can truly define good; man does not have the ability to differentiate lasting good from evil. He must bless Hashem constantly, for whatever comes his way.

Rabbi Eliezer Papo would recommend that after making requests of Hashem, we conclude with the following prayer:

"Do for us what is good in Your eyes for Your service, which will find favor before the heavenly throne. Rectify our spirit and soul and gladden the heart of Your servant, for we look to You our G-d and trust only in You." (Bais Tefillah)

Prayer at All Times

As we face the demands of our daily existence, we must constantly pray for success, knowing that there is no correlation between our efforts in the material world and our achievements.[81] Regular impromptu prayer reinforces our knowledge that there is no such thing as chance.[82] Such prayer compensates for the prayers said by rote from the *siddur*.[83] A constant preoccupation with prayer ensures that we avoid sinning.[84]

Every profit and every joy in this world is from Hashem. Our sages said, "If only a person would daven all day long!" *(Berachos 21,1)* But how will such a person study Torah and take care of all his needs? R' Yosef Chaim of Baghdad explains that the *Gemara* is referring to our focus throughout the day.

Let us visualize a craftsman whose tools and materials are laid out before him and who has just begun to assemble the final product. He must not conclude, "I am all set, nothing can prevent me from completing my task." He should think, "If Hashem does not endow me with life and vigor I can do nothing." As long as he is working, his thoughts should be turned to Hashem in silent prayer that he be permitted to finish the job.

When a person is traveling down a well-paved route towards his objective, he should not conclude that he is certain to arrive at his destination. He should pray to Hashem that nothing prevent him from getting where he wishes to go. If tasty food has been placed before him and he is about to lift the spoon to his mouth, he should *daven* to Hashem that he be able to swallow and that his digestive system operate smoothly.[85]

Before entering into a business venture, we should recite the following short prayer: "Master of the Universe, in your holy Scriptures it says, 'One who trusts in Hashem shall be surrounded by kindness' *(Tehillim 32,10)* and 'You sustain everything' *(Nechemiyah 9,2).* Give me, out of your kindness, a blessing in this venture I am about to do." When one is successful in a venture he should say, "With the help of G–d I was successful."[86]

The *Gemara* advises that before a person sets foot in a city, he should pray to Hashem that he enter in peace. Before he leaves he should pray that he leave unscathed.[87]

R' Yechezkel Abramsky was a proponent of spontaneous prayer. He was once sitting at his table where he studied and wrote, when he suddenly he looked out the window and started to cry. He called out, "Master of the world, until when will there be no rain? Have compassion on Your children."

Before leaving his house, R' Yechezkel would touch the mezuzah and request that Hashem enable him to return in good health. (Pninei R' Yechezkel)

Praying Before Tragedy Strikes

R' Yitzchok bar R' Yehuda said, "A person should always daven that he not fall ill, for when a person is sick, the Heavenly court convenes to determine if he is worthy of being cured." *(Shabbos 32a)*

R' Elazar said, "Always pray before tragedy strikes. If Avraham had not offered a prayer between Bais El and Ai, then nothing would remain of the Jewish people today." *(Sanhedrin 44)* Avraham anticipated the future and prayed that his descendants be spared.

In a small European shtetl not far from a border, a group of smugglers conceived of an original method of trafficking goods across the border. On one side of the border there was an old cemetery, used by people on both sides. Officials agreed that the deceased could be buried in their respective plots, despite the border. Funeral processions were permitted to cross the border undisturbed.

The smugglers took advantage of this situation by staging mock funerals in which the caskets were filled with contraband goods and carried across the border by a special entourage. All went well until one day one of the border guards pointed out that certain funerals seemed rather unemotional. He wondered why no crying accompanied some of the deceased. The next time this silent group asked to pass the border, the guards asked that the casket be opened. Crying and moaning could be heard from all sides, but to no avail.

The officials said, "Now it is too late to cry. If you had cried before, you would not have been suspected, and everything would have proceeded in an orderly fashion. But since you didn't cry then, your crying now will have no effect."

Most people call out to Hashem only when calamity strikes. But it is much easier to mitigate a punishment before a verdict is passed.

How can a person pray to avoid a tragedy he cannot even anticipate? He should always try to pray with sincerity, and repent as soon as he can after committing a sin. When beginning a potentially dangerous project or entering a threatening environment, prayers should be increased. R' Chaim of Volozhin endorsed the concept of praying for protection when a person is exposed to spiritual temptation.

Yaakov Avinu serves as a prototype for this approach. He prayed on Binyamin's behalf before he left for Mitzrayim, as he instinctively felt that his youngest son would be exposed to danger there.[88]

In Vilna, the Chazon Ish and his wife lived in a two-room apartment. One room served as living quarters and the other was a store where his wife sold material. Business was not good. Although there were a lot of customers who inconvenienced the Rebbetzin, there was little profit and she accumulated many debts. Years after they settled in Eretz Yisrael, the Chazon Ish was still paying his creditors.

To compound their difficulties, the Rebbetzin had to deal

with a gentile who was a rabid anti-Semite. He accused her of stealing a portion of his inventory and informed the authorities. He even hired false witnesses to testify against her. When she received the summons to appear in court, the Rebbetzin realized she was in grave trouble. She had no witnesses who could testify on her behalf and she was likely to be severely punished. She was overcome with fear.

The Chazon Ish asked for the wicked gentile's name. He stood in a corner and poured out his heart before his Father in Heaven to save them from the consequences of this dastardly act. Several days before the court date, the gentile died and the litigation was canceled.

After the death of her husband, a mother asked her son if he could explain a note she had discovered among his father's papers. The son explained that twelve years earlier his father had sent him to the Steipler to discuss his concerns at the premature deaths of his three brothers. The Steipler had advised him to always say the Yom Kippur Katan prayers.

When his mother heard that she paled and began to tremble. "Now I understand," she exclaimed. "He was always very careful to say the Yom Kippur Katan prayers even if he was unwell. This past Rosh Chodesh, when I heard him bentching, I reminded him to say Yaaleh VeYavo. He seemed horrified. After he finished, he commented that he had forgotten to say the Yom Kippur Katan prayers. He added sorrowfully that this was the first time that he had missed the *prayers of Yom Kippur Katan in twelve years."*

When the story was repeated to the Steipler, he said it was well known that Yom Kippur Katan prayers help annul evil decrees. He had made the suggestion because he feared that the siblings had died because of an evil decree.

The Steipler advised the administration of the Mir Yeshiva in America to recite the Yom Kippur Katan prayers after a number of their students died prematurely. After their first Yom Kippur Katan session, the deaths miraculously stopped. *(Koheles Yaakov)*

Praying Everywhere

"Tremble and do not sin, say it in your heart and on your bed." *(Tehillim 4,5)* Hashem instructed the Jewish people to pray in a shul. If this is not possible, they should pray in the field; otherwise, in their houses. And if they cannot pray in the house, they should pray on their beds. If praying on the bed is out of the question, they should at least meditate in their hearts.

As the Zohar says, "There is no good resolution that is lost. Hashem collects them all. Therefore blessed is he who thinks positive thoughts and connects to the Creator of the world." *(Part II 150,20)*

A person should pray constantly and everywhere – in the field and in his house, on the road and at home. One should regularly ponder Hashem's greatness and turn to Him at every opportunity for all things large and small.[89]

When righteous people say the words, *im yirtzeh Hashem* (G–d willing), it is a verbalized prayer that Hashem help them succeed. *Baruch Hashem* (thank G–d) is a prayer of thankfulness.[89]

There is a special channel to Hashem when *davening* at *mekomos kedoshim* (holy sites). *Tzaddikim* would send representatives to daven for them at holy sites when they could not make the trip personally.

When informed that someone was sick, the Brisker Rav, Maharil Diskin, would daven immediately. One day he received a message from Europe to pray on behalf of the grandson of one of the Kollel benefactors, who had been called to serve in the army. He asked R' Zevulun Charlap to organize a minyan at the Kosel immediately, asking Hashem to exempt the young man from the draft. The minyan recited Tehillim and then davened the evening prayer. When they finished, they reported back to the Brisker Rav. He asked that they organize one more public prayer for this cause. A few weeks later, they received a letter from the philanthropist, joyously informing them that his grandson was freed from army service. (Amud Aish)

Rabbi Nachum Rabinowitz, a respected Yerushalmi, was once summoned by the Belzer Rebbe. When R' Nachum entered, R' Aharon asked his forgiveness for troubling him, but added that he had a request. "I would very much like to visit the Kosel at least once a week, but the trip is very difficult for me. I would like to appoint you as my representative to visit the Kosel when I ask you to do so. When you arrive at the wall, you should say my name and the name of my mother, and apologize on my behalf for being unable to visit the Kosel in person."

When R' Nachum asked the Rebbe how many chapters of Tehillim he should say, the Rebbe answered, "As you please. One chapter is all right. You can say the whole book of Tehillim if you wish. When you complete your portion of Tehillim, say my name again and add 'Aharon son of Basya Ruchama asks the Holy One, Blessed be He, that all his blessings for all Jews be fulfilled.'"

From that day on, from 5706 through 5708 (1946-1948), R' Nachum was sent to the Kosel once or twice a week by the Rebbe. (Hischazkus BeTefillah LaHashem, page 85)

When the Rav of Brisk was deathly ill, R' Yaakov Yisrael Kanievsky went to Meron to pray on his behalf. When he was informed that his condition had deteriorated, he decided to visit the grave of his brother-in-law, the Chazon Ish. When he arrived with his entourage, they found the gate locked. Determined to pray under all circumstances, he scaled the fence, approached the grave and started to pray. (Toldos Yaakov)

As poor as he was, R' Yehoshua Tzvi Michel Shapira would pay numerous indigents to say Tehillim on his behalf each day. When the Maharil Diskin, also known as the Brisker Rav, wanted to appoint him head of the Suvalk Kollel, R' Yehoshua Tzvi Michel hired people to go to the Kosel and other holy places to pray that he be spared this honor. The Brisker Rav soon forgot about this idea.

May the prayers of these great men serve as an inspiration to us so that the sum total of our prayers bring Moshiach immediately.

[1] Shemos 32:11

[2] Beraishis 48:22

[3] Beraishis 25:21

[4] Shmuel I, Chapter 1

[5] Bereishis 25,23

[6] Shmuel II 24:25

[7] Divrei HaYamim 2,32

[8] Melachim 2,20

[9] Taanis 19a

[10] Yismach Yisrael, page 23

[11] Emes LeYaakov Taanis, page 2

[12] Yevamos 105

[13] Pnei David

[14] Yaaros Devash, lecture 5

[15] Sefer HaChassidim 131

[16] Matnas Chaim, R' Matisyahu Solomon

[17] Ruach Chaim, Avos Chapter 3, Mishnah 4

[18] Siddur HaGra, Introduction

[19] Matnas Chaim, R' Matisyahu Solomon

[20] Sanhedrin, Mishnah 6

[21] Shir HaShirim 5,2

[22] Likutei Amarim, chapter 10

[23] Nefesh HaChaim gate two, chapter 11 and chapter 12

[24] Derasha of R' Chaim of Volozhin

[25] Midrash Shochar Tov, 13

[26] Magid Devarav LeYaakov

[27] Sefer HaYirah

[28] Yaaros Devash, Part I, Derush 1

[29] Adapted from Daas Chochmah U'Mussar, Part II

[30] Macos 11

[31] Midrash Pinchas

[32] Sefer HaChassidim 553

[33] Bereishis 20,17; see Rashi

[34] Iyov 42:8

[35] Bais Elokim, Tefillah page 12, 15b

[36] Marpeh Lashon, Pillar of Service

[37] Beer Moshe, Ekev

[38] Mishnas Rebbe Aharon

[39] Binah LeItim, Lecture 2 on Tefillah

[40] Shmuel I 12:23

[41] Bamidbar 35:11-12

[42] Macos 11; Levush in Levush Ha'orah

[43] Bava Basra 116

[44] Shearim BeTefillah, Kriah

[45] Sichos Chochmah U'Mussar I, Makos 1,1

[46] Likutei Torah Taamei Hamitzvos, Vayikra

[47] Kav HaYashar, Chapter 5

[48] Reb Pinchas Koretz, Midrash Pinchas 21

[49] Mesilas Yesharim 19

[50] Od Yosef Chai

[51] Midrash Pesikta Rabasi 20

[52] Berachos 10a

[53] Zohar, Part I, 105,1

[54] R' Chasdai Crescas, Or Hashem 3b 1

[55] Mofes HaDor

[56] Yaaros Devash Part I, Derush 1

[57] Rosh on Nedarim 40,1

[58] Bamidbar Rabbah 22,3

[59] R' Ephraim Zaitchek

[60] Ahavas Chesed, chapter 8

61 Correspondence, part II, letter 123

62 Sifsei Chaim 3,354

63 Or Elchonon 2,171

64 Mofes Hador

65 Chayei Olam, chapter 28

66 Yaaros Devash Derush 1, page 13

67 Midrash Vayikra Rabbah 5,8

68 Zohar 169a

69 Kuntres HaTzavaah

70 Sefer Chassidim, chapter 158; Derech Chaim

71 Avos 2,18

72 Chasdei Avos

73 Rokeach, page 9

74 Bais Avrohom, 13

75 Chassam Sofer, part III, page 19, Tur 2

76 Michtav MeEliyahu, part II

77 HaKesav VeHaKabalah Devarim 26,4

78 Adapted from Sefer HaIkarim, Essay 4, chapter 24

79 Birchas Aharon, chapter 4 on Berachos, letter 249

80 M. Berachos 9,1

81 Michtav MeEliyahu

82 Meor VeShemesh

83 Likutei Amarim 10

84 Yaaros Devash, Derush 1

85 Benayahu, Berachos 6

86 Shaloh HaKadosh on Tefillah 2,217a

87 Berachos 60, see page 47 Hischazkus BeTefillah LaHashem

88 Bereishis 43,14

89 Be'er Moshe, Ekev

90 ibid